AYAHUASCA

HEALING YOUR SOUL

by
Liam Browne
2019

www.liambrowne.com

AYAHUASCA

HEALING YOUR SOUL

by
Liam Browne
2019

Some names have been changed to protect the privacy of family and friends.

Copyright © Liam Browne 2019
All rights reserved

This book or any portion thereof may not be reproduced or used in any manner whatsoever without the express written permission of the author except for the use of brief quotations in line with copyright law.

Cover Design by Libertine Design
Edited by Johanna Craven
Proofread & Formatted by Evelyn Kristen Hills

A FREE 'UNPUBLISHED' POEM FOR YOU!

As a massive thank you for buying this book, I would like to give you a little present. This is only for you, the people who have supported my work. I hope my experience has opened your mind to spirituality and given you something to think about.

This is a poem I recite from time to time in my yoga classes. It seems to really resonate with people. They always say it gives them a sense of hope. It came to me in savasana in a yoga class. I couldn't get out of the class fast enough as it was fully formed in me head. I needed to write it down quickly before I forgot it.

Always know something good is coming from all negative situations. It is our task to stay as passive as possible to the dark and the light. To be non-reactive. Magnificence is waiting around the corner. Move beyond you imagined limitations.

You can download it here - www.liambrowne.com/embrace

CONTENTS

Chapter 1, Answering The Call 13

Chapter 2, The Terror 37

Chapter 3, All The Blessings 62

Free Poem 89

Also by Liam Browne 90

Acknowledgements & Gratitude 91

Sample Chapter 95

Bibliography 101

Links 103

Always for you, Mum

IQUITOS, PERU
2013

CHAPTER 1
ANSWERING THE CALL

Sitting in my tin roof hut in the middle of the Amazon rainforest, my feet felt like they were on fire from itchiness. It was almost pitch black, I was writing sitting on a small wooden chair by candlelight. I'd delicately placed a candle on a small stool beside me, strategically manoeuvred, ensuring minimum shadow from hand and pen onto page. I was somewhere between Iquitos and Nakula in the north of Peru in the north-west part of the Amazon. I was about to embark on a spiritual journey I had been looking forward to for over eighteen months.

Ayahuasca is seen as the world's most powerful psychedelic, enabling those thirsty enough to experience other dimensions of reality, past lives and a realisation of what comes after death. It is only administered by experienced shamans who have studied the plants and the places they take you for many years. Iquitos has the reputation of being the World HQ for such practices and was beyond doubt the main reason for my visit to Peru and the focus of my journey to the Americas.

Earlier in my travels when I was in Belize, I had been told about a fantastic lady called Otillia, who lived at Kilometre 51, between Iquitos and Nakula. I found out about her from a French couple at the start of my trip. I told them of my desire to experience Ayahuasca, and they said that Otillia was one of the best. They'd drunk Ayahuasca with her and had had the most beautiful experience. They gave me the contacts of a friend called Bruno who lived in Iquitos and was something of an Ayahuasca connoisseur. They all firmly believed that Otillia was one of the most authentic in the whole of Peru. I had thought I was going to have to do a lot of research and digging around to find a good shaman, so I felt completely blessed that within the first two weeks of my trip I had resolved that little dilemma.

After a few messages to Greg and Marie, I made contact with Bruno and headed to Iquitos with fellow travellers Rule, Livika and Tank. We arrived late after almost a day and a half of travelling from Cusco. We booked into a floating hostel and saw a monkey riding a dog.

That evening we ate at a place called The Yellow Rose of Texas, apparently owned by an American guy — not from Texas — who didn't speak a word of Spanish after living here for twenty years.

The Yellow Rose offered an Ayahuasca menu, which stated at the top of the page, NO SALT, NO SUGAR, NO OIL and NO SEX. My internal child chuckled away at the fact that the dish I'd ordered categorically contained no sex. I didn't want to break the sabbatical I had been on for the last five months. I'd realised I had a problem when it came to sex. I couldn't be faithful, and I couldn't look at beautiful women without my sexual appetite rearing its head. I'd started to work with energy, and I knew the sexual part of me needed some work. I wanted to stop giving off this sexual vibe. I wanted to be able to control myself.

So yes, no sex and no masturbation for that long.

Where does that unused fluid go?

Those who know me wouldn't believe it or fathom how I could do it as it was the longest I had gone without since I'd started twenty years ago. It actually wasn't much of a challenge, and I was surprised at the way I seemed to be able to concentrate a lot better and not be constantly distracted by the people around me.

Iquitos seemed like a pretty big city, and it was crazy to think we were days from anywhere. After my dull, bland, dry meal, I went to bed, excited to see what the Amazon looked like the next morning in the light of day.

I awoke to see the splendour of the jungle; its still, lush waters, serenely supporting an array of floating plant life, the constant croaking of frogs and the small splashes as its rich content of fish sprang to the surface. It was something stunning and beautiful, something I'd always dreamt of seeing. It was like I was in a trippy dream, mesmerised by the extreme mass of flowing water and the richness it carried. I sat and watched as next to me, a monkey chased a dog.

I was starting to worry. I hadn't contacted Bruno. I wanted to get to Otillia as fast as I could. That was the only reason I was here; inner work, inner work I kept telling myself.

I emailed Bruno, and the next day, I had a reply with a place and time to meet to begin my Ayahuasca journey. Rule was interested in trying Ayahuasca as a drug tourist rather than for a specific reason. He had told me about the cocaine bar he had been to in Bolivia where you get a table and can order as much cocaine as you want. This would have really appealed to me a few years ago. At the height of my drug use, I had often dreamt of going to South America and taking proper un-cut cocaine. However, Rule and Livika had booked to go on an Amazon boat tour for a few days, and it was now Tank who was interested in joining me for the ceremony.

I'd read so much about the preparation for Ayahuasca ceremonies; the diet, the intention, and being ready mentally. To me, Rule and Tank were neither of those things, they just wanted an experience. For me it was more than that, it was a spiritual experience, one that I'd prepared for and put so much emphasis on for so long. I felt like I'd earnt it. I believed you had to respect Ayahuasca, getting out what you put in. If you didn't, it would just be like another recreational drug experience. Ayahuasca isn't a drug and, from what I'd read, is not something you can just do at the weekend as an escape. It is never done alone, always in groups and always with a doctor or shaman with the right training.

Tank wanted to be free of his ten-year prescription drug reliance but seemed unwilling to make any effort or changes to make this a reality. I don't feel like there is an easy fix to change, you have to get rid of other stuff. It's a really difficult thing as we see it as part of our identity. They say that Ayahuasca can achieve in a few hours what thirty years of therapy could possibly resolve with slow integration. It allows you to become aware of the actual problem and then slowly find a way to get past it.

This got my creative juices flowing, and when thinking about my process of not going down the prescription drug route, I came up with this poem that summarised a realisation I had when coming to terms with depression and getting over my anger issues:

Change
Until we realise we are the problem
Our lives will remain in limbo
Full of anger, fear and darkness
Until we realise that the situations
And people we think hurt us
Are exactly what we have chosen
We will remain trapped in sadness
Change your world, Change your life

We couldn't meet Otillia until the next morning.

Tank was still interested, and I was actually thinking it may do him some good, considering the amount of time he had been on pills. He was worried about the side effects of mixing the Ayahuasca. He was over-intellectualising the situation and was full of questions for Otillia and Bruno. I just sat, smile and nod, smile and nod, I thought.

Tank sought advice from all quarters; his neurologist, counsellor and doctor, all of course warning against this unknown entity which actually pre-dates any form of western medicine, is completely natural and known to have astonishingly high success rates in so many areas.

I assumed none of these professionals had had any experience with such practices, so how on Earth could they warn someone against it? It's like me warning someone against anal sex when I've never had it myself.

Ayahuasca is supposed to induce enhanced states of awareness, perception and cognition, areas that can help many illnesses, especially in terms of mental health. Ayahuasca gives drinkers their own tools to overcome problems and a heightened consciousness; a consciousness that could, in some ways, threaten the materialistic western society. Surely if these scientists and sceptics actually participated in these practices or studied the effects on the consciousness of other participants, they would be deemed more credible when vilifying such traditions. Their current method of analysis seems more like asking an elderly person to describe raving in a nightclub.

Western science only figured out the complex chemistry of Ayahuasca a few decades ago and as J.C. Callaway states: *'it is, without doubt, one of the most sophisticated and complex drug delivery systems in existence.'*

Staying in the hostel with us was a very stereotypical American ex-pat. He had quite a square shape to him, a little bit stocky, with a deep gravelly voice. His hair seemed military issue, and due to his age, which I suspected to be around fifty, there was a lot of grey. His combat shorts and plain double-pocketed shirt finished off his look.

I think his name was Rod, but it could have been Chad, Brad, Ron or Chuck. He'd travelled a lot, and had horror stories from everywhere he had been. He warned us against this place and that told us about a French bloke who got robbed by the police in Panama. I told him about how I'd been to a scary part of town (which tourists are told to avoid) without a guide a few days earlier, and he thought I was crazy.

I said, 'That stuff don't happen to me, man.'

He said, 'So what, you're not a fucking gringo? Your white skin ain't saying "rob me I have money"?'

I said, 'No, I don't think it does, mate. I've been in lots of situations on my travels where I was in the worst places and around people who could have robbed me, but it never happened".

He just laughed and said, 'Well you're living in a fucking dream world, man.'

I thought, yes I am, and my dream world doesn't include your bullshit. Why would I include that in my world?

'I'm always looking out and being careful, knowing some motherfucker is lurking around the corner to rob me,' he said.

Of course, you are because you are looking for it, you usually find what you're looking for if you look hard enough, I thought. How frightfully miserable and on edge your life must be, constantly manifesting bad situations.

Obviously, he was warning Tank off the Ayahuasca as much as possible. I really wanted to be out of this man's space. The negativity, the fear and aggression he carried, were very unattractive to the new me, but he was a character, so I observed him a while longer, thinking I could possibly use some of his traits if I was ever asked to play someone like this in a movie. I tried not to add much to the conversation and keep the guy's negative energy from having any effect on me.

We were due to leave for Otillia's place that morning, but there were riots and demonstrations all over Iquitos, so Otillia said she would be back at 4pm to take us to the jungle. Apparently, the president had taken some backhanders, so the streets were all blocked. It looked like a war zone outside. Gone was the madness of traffic and people selling stuff. The roads were now empty but for rubble and garbage scattered everywhere with groups of thugs going around smashing things up.

We were told we would leave that evening when the trouble died down.

We were hostel-bound, we couldn't go out. Apparently, this was the first time this had ever happened, so in a way I felt privileged to be privy to such excitement. We were told we would leave at four, but four came and went, so did six, then Otillia called, saying she would collect us the next morning.

By this time Tank had opted out, saying too much weird stuff had happened. We had been held hostage in the hostel all day. The hostel owner was Brazilian and seemed to love drama. He said Otillia would not return for us.

I knew she would.

In this part of the world, it was nothing to be ten days late. Some places take weeks to get to, so a few days here and there is probably the equivalent of a few seconds in the west.

With Tank being from the epitome of westernisation, where nothing is waited for, this minor delay threw his customer complaint mind into overdrive.

Otillia turned up at the hostel at 8am, not at 11am as the dramatic Brazilian had relayed. I had an idea he may have been lying to add drama to the situation.

I was whisked off with Otillia.

After forty minutes, we were dropped at a bench, and Otillia pointed me towards a clearing in the jungle. I had no idea what she was saying, but I understood that she wanted me to walk into the jungle for about thirty minutes. It was a small cleared path, and I had no idea where I was going. I wondered why she wasn't coming with me. Was this some kind of test, did I have to win her trust by walking for thirty minutes and realising there was nothing and returning? I had faith I was doing the right thing, and after thirty minutes I come to a clearing where I was greeted by a small man in a boiler suit who pointed me towards a wooden cabin.

The large opening in the jungle had bright-coloured flowers growing everywhere. The grounds were lush, and a main large wooden house was situated in the middle and several cabins were dotted around the grounds. I was shown to my room, which was a small wooden hut with a beautiful mosquito net covered bed in a nice room with hammock and toilet. It was basic but what else would I need? I was taken to the Commodore, which was a large long table where you eat meals and was covered with mosquito netting with a natural palm roof. I was given breakfast and my first plant medicine which tasted like garlic. I had no idea what I was drinking, my trust and health were now fully in the hands of Otillia and her team.

I lazily lay in the hammock hour after hour until I was called for dinner. It was so interesting, to be so relaxed and so at peace with doing nothing. My mind was completely blank, which already felt like a massive breakthrough. I stared at my foot and the surrounding jungle canopy with very little else going on in my mind.

The next day I would be fully emerged and participating in an age-old tradition, one that I felt would change my life forever. I was very, very excited but at the same time, the unknown and something new brought an element of fear.

I'd opted for a seven-day *Dieta* (diet) (Ayahuasca Retreat) under the care of Otillia, which consisted of a plant-based diet and two or three Ayahuasca ceremonies. The *Dieta* can last for seven, ten, or fifteen days or between one and three months, and you can work with a single or a few plants. I would be working with one plant called Ajo Sacha, which would work with specific problems I had with knees and other joints as well as depression and an array of mental problems and past trauma.

The diet you partake in is used to cleanse the system and should be started at least a week before your retreat. It includes abstaining from red meat and pork and cutting back on chicken and fish. You have to eliminate salt, pepper and most other spices (especially hot spices like chilli), sugar including most desserts and pastries, and fats and oils are banned. You're not allowed any prescription medicines, especially those that act as MAO inhibitors (Monoamine oxidase inhibitors) or are tranquillisers or anti-depressants. They also don't want you having yeast products, fermented foods such as soya or tofu, pickled foods, acidic foods, citrus and dairy products. Alcohol and coffee are prohibited, as are tea and other caffeine-rich drinks. One must abstain from sex and masturbation, and no iced or cold drinks are allowed. Everything you put on or in your body must be natural, including toothpastes and soaps.

The diet is essential so that the plants can have the best possible chance of doing what they are supposed to do. Because the diet contains no flavour, your sense of smell is said to become more sensitive, your body and its smell changes, your sight gets better, and your piss becomes clear. It has the same results as a fast in many ways, creating the perfect vessel for the plants to do what they are supposed to do, finding the space prepared for them to work. You are ingesting the spirit of the plant, and that is the medicine that works with you. Ayahuasca is the glamour plant, the best known, its name attracts like Tiger Woods at a golf tournament or The Beatles in their day at an airport.

Healers in Peru always use Ayahuasca in conjunction with other plants and the special diet is just as important as the Ayahuasca ceremony itself. However, Ayahuasca's spirit is seen as the top of the hierarchy, it being the mother of all plants.

After my food and plant medicine, I lay in Otillia's living room, reading of all things, a book from her bookshelf about British stylist Gok Wan and his upbringing in Nottingham. As I was doing this, Otillia was sewing. She was quite short with what looked like a mix of Inca and Spanish blood, she must have been in her fifties or sixties, but could actually have been older. She did have a few grandchildren flying about so who knows? She looked like any other grandmother catching up with some craftwork, but tomorrow I thought, this grandma will be administering me one of the most powerful hallucinogenics on the planet.

After I returned to my cabin for a few hours, I was summoned to follow one of Otillia's assistants towards a little blue conventional bath buried in the ground, its contents filled with the most beautiful collection of flower buds and petals. I undressed and readied myself to plunge into my first ever flower bath. A piece of tarp was attached to sticks to block out the sun and the rain. I submerged myself, feeling pampered like never before.

The aroma sent my nostrils into overdrive, as they frantically tried to label and savour these divine scents. As I took in the jungle canopy around me, I listened to the constant sound of crickets, frogs, birds, chickens and insects. A warm, loving feeling soaked through my whole body, and I felt the cleansing effects manifest immediately.

I retired for the evening and sat down to write. I had no idea of the date, time or day of the week. Actually I was pretty unsure of the last time I'd had any recollection of these things. A little while later two white men came into my hut. They introduced themselves as Dave and Ferdinand and told me Otillia would like to know if I would like to join them in ceremony that evening?

"Of course", I said, and Dave said he would collect me when it was time.

It seemed out of the blue.

I felt unprepared.

I thought that my first ceremony would be the next evening, but I had no second thoughts. This was what I was here for. I was excited to experience this age-old tradition and started to think about what would be in store for me. In Joan Parisi Wilcox's book, *AYAHUASCA-The Visionary and Healing Powers of the Vine of the Soul*, she states that *"one must be prepared for the terror and to have enough practice in maintaining one's centre before embarking on such a journey. One thing is certain about the vine, there is no telling what you will get, but it will definitely be what you need"*. I was hoping all the meditation, yoga and personal development I'd done over the last year would stand me in good stead, and I would be able to stay centred.

Dave arrived, and we made our way to Otillia's wooden hut, which doubled up as the ceremonial space. One candle sat on a bookshelf, just about illuminating the space. It felt like somewhere completely different to the room I'd been lay in reading earlier.

Otillia sat in the same chair she had been sewing in but was now dressed in a full-length ceremonial robe, colourful flowered patterns adorning the crisp white material flowing down to the floor. In front of her was a small knee-high table with various bits of paraphernalia on it, which I couldn't really make out due to the dim light. Otillia sat in her chair and waved at me to be seated. Spaces had been prepared, folded mattresses were placed against the wooden walls awaiting our arrival. Each mattress had its own bowl which I assumed was for when the purging began.

I took the space to Otillia's left, close to the door in case I needed to escape to the bathroom, as I had heard you could be violently sick from both ends.

Dave sat facing Otillia, and Ferdinand sat to Otillia's left but slightly behind. Ferdinand seemed very experienced and was talking us through the process. He said that once you have drunk, you should try to keep the brew down for as long as possible and stay as upright as you can with a straight spine throughout the whole experience. He said that when you drink Ayahuasca, you should keep your heart open, and try and be led by your heart, not your head. He then told us that just as you are about to drink, you should make an intention for the ceremony. What is it you want to be shown? What areas do you feel you need guidance with and what needs to be healed?

We all sat cross-legged in our spaces. I had few butterflies in my stomach, a giddy excitement filled me. Otillia pulled a plastic bottle from a bag that contained a dark coloured liquid which I assumed was the brew. She said some words or prayers as she lit some tobacco. She then opened the top of the bottle and blew smoke inside it three times. She then blew smoke around the bottle three times. Next, she stood and went around to each of us, blowing tobacco smoke around our heads and bodies. She asked for our hands and blew smoke into our palms three times. She sat down and performed a few more rituals and poured the first cup of Ayahuasca, blowing smoke three times into the brew and then beckoning Dave with a stern call of, "Señor". I watched him approach and kneel before Otillia, accept the cup, internally setting his intentions and knocking back the brew. I studiously watched so I wouldn't mess up my turn. Otillia gave him some tissue to wipe his mouth, and he returned to his mat. Nervous energy engulfed me as I knew I was next. She filled the bowl again, blowing the tobacco around it three times and called "Señor," beckoning me forward. I knew what I wanted to ask now. I looked at Otillia as she handed me the bowl and a radiant glow now surrounded her face. I knew what I wanted to ask, "show me my heart and give me direction".

I'd been through a lot over the last few years, and there was so much I wanted to try and process. There was the death of my mother and the way it had affected me. There was my inability to commit to relationships. There was the fact I felt I could still have a future with the girl I had broken up with three months ago. There was the fact I had been dealing and taking a lot of drugs. The fact I had just about avoided prison. More than anything, there was the fact I was living in the body of a very lost and troubled man who felt he had no purpose. I really wanted to know what my purpose was. I had written a list a few days earlier of things I wanted to ask, but it just ended up huge. They were: direction, Mum, life purpose, spiritual direction/growth, focus, knowing my own mind, remembering, home/family/life, knee pain, work, place, diet, body pain, friendship, Fhian, what am I here for, where to find happiness, Mum, commitment, family, destiny, stability, home, life's calling, find my place, work, lessons I have to learn, Fhian, headspace, shoulder pain, calf pain, ability to relax, knees, connecting to higher self, connecting to guides, divinity, destiny, spiritual life path, healing, happiness/direction, home/happiness, soul plan, higher purpose, higher self, abundance in everything, creativity, guitar playing, priorities, focus, language of light, yoga direction, building practices, and clear direction. Just a couple of things I wanted help with, but I stuck with being shown my heart.

I knelt down before Otillia. She poured the brew and handed me the small wooden bowl that seemed to be a carved and polished coconut shell. The smell immediately hit me; a thick earthy foul pong swirled up my nostrils, connecting with my brain. I was trying to process what this unusual smell was. I looked at the brew, at my first experience with Ayahuasca, set my intention for the ceremony, asking to be shown what my heart wanted, to be led by my heart and be given direction. I glugged back the dark brown thick liquid in one gulp. I was given tissue and then headed back to what would be my station for the next five or so hours. The Ayahuasca tasted foul, worse than anything I'd ever tasted before. It was so thick, not gloopy but an even consistency and the taste was like a swamp or rotting vegetation. I was actually expecting worse from the stories I'd been told, but still, it was foul.

I crossed my legs. I didn't feel sick, which was what I was expecting, and the liquid seemed to go down quite well. I sat in my lotus pose and watched Ferdinand take his brew.

Otillia took hers and then blew out the candle.

In the darkness, I was able to see the outline of people's bodies illuminated by the faint moonlight.

I waited for the effects.

Fifteen minutes in, Dave began to purge. For some reason, my ego was glad I wasn't the first to go. I was feeling fine. Dave retched for a few minutes, and I thought 'has he had the Ayahuasca in his system long enough for it to take effect?' Another ten minutes passed, and Ferdinand vomited, and my ego was gleaming. For some reason in this situation my competitive side was shining through, I felt happy and strong that I had held it down for so long. But what did that actually mean? I knew it didn't matter.

Visualisations were starting to form. With my eyes shut, geometric shapes were creating a black and white kaleidoscope in my mind; beautiful triangular patterns were morphing into other patterns, circles, hexagons, squares all bursting into each other with flawless grace.

All of a sudden, I reached for my bucket and was sick a few times from the bottom of my guts. It brought me to my knees over the bowl as it all came out. I wiped my mouth and sat back down to regain my composure. As I closed my eyes, I discovered that colour had erupted into my elegant, stylised visuals. I got comfortable again, ready to enjoy the show. Reds, greens and blues added texture and vividness to the shape shown. Sequences evolved into patterns and patterns into vast shapes and landscapes made up of triangles. It felt like the trippy hallucinogenic scene in the Disney film *Dumbo*, but a million times more beautiful.

I was expecting harder visions, I was expecting people, spirits objects to come to me, I was expecting to be catapulted into another dimension. I was seeing these patterns I had never seen before. It's very hard to explain what I was seeing, to have the vocabulary to fully describe what was going on in my head. It was stunning, dazzling, beautiful and sublime, and part of me wanted to experience it forever.

As the visions became more and more complex, Otillia started to sing and shake her rattle, her *Icaro's* (songs) providing another layer of beauty to this already dreamy world I was in. The *Icaro's* took me on a little journey, and when she shook the rattle, the visions would splatter and dissipate like she was shaking the delicate kaleidoscope in my mind each time the rattle moved. I opened my eyes, and the patterns in my mind were now all over the room. I could see the outline of the two guys and could see the figure of Otillia in front of me. She was rocking back and forth on her rocking chair as she'd done whilst sewing. The way Joan Parisi Wilcox describes her visions was very similar to what I was seeing; *"I was assaulted by geometry, looming before me were huge spheres, dense and darkly hued, they formed complex patterns, spinning in ways so intricate I could barely fathom their movements, the immensity was overwhelming even terrifying"*

Nail on the head. I actually felt good in myself, calm, happy, serene, blissful. The images of my life started to show a future of love and happiness. It was showing me simplicity and simplicity was the focus. It was showing me love, confirming what I had felt for the last four months. It showed me Fhian, it showed me I needed nothing more, everything was with her. It showed the two of us together forever, it showed me that all we needed was love, love is all you need. We were holding a baby, I was the happiest man alive, and the radiance that shone from Fhian's being was the most beautiful I'd ever seen in my life. There was a baby and us. That was all we needed. Family close by, a few good friends, but more than anything, each other, that was all that mattered.

Lady Ayahuasca kept me focused on simplicity and showing people how to live free by doing it myself. I was building a house for me and Fhian in Chorlton, Manchester. I was converting a garage in someone's garden into a one-room starter home for us to start a family in, a cosy love nest, with a loft bed incorporating the sustainable principles I'd learnt and making it our own. Enticing her with the blissful setting I'd created. I was shown this was my dream. This was the most important thing, no more travelling after this until I'd created a home for us both. I was shown all the construction methods to use, how to maximise space.

The building was full of love, full of Fhian and Liam, everything else took a back seat. There was a small garden with a white picket fence, the garage door had been replaced with glazing facing south to maximise solar gain, and a beautiful free-standing Victorian bath sat in the garden with a shower curtain around it, looking both decorative and functional. We also had a drop toilet around the side using a septic tank, and blissfully we sat with friends around a fire pit made from glass bottles. I sat there with my head resting on my knee in pure bliss. I wanted Fhian to see the smile on my face, the contentedness, the love we had, the love we had brought each other and the love the baby had brought. I sat holding our baby and her, knowing this was all life was about, making this happen, everything else just seemed like meaningless rubbish.

I wanted to show her, tell her, let her experience this feeling, know her opinion. We were so in love, it would have made some people a little sick. The feeling was intense, it was like she was with me, holding me, sharing this feeling with me.

We then started this business and a community of people turning garages into small homes. I got a message that said, "Why do people have buildings to house their cars when there are people without homes?"

I thought about this couple I had met on my travels in Taos who had lived in this tiny hut for two years. They were both over six foot six, he was an ex-international volleyball player and her, an ex-international basketball player. They'd had their first child in this tiny space, and it had spent the first eighteen months of its life there. Now they had this huge three-bed Earthship, and the hut was used as storage space.

In the vision, it was my mission to turn as many garages into homes as possible, showing people an alternative way to live, to own your own life. The Ayahuasca said do this, and your love will come to you, create a home for you both. I then had a vision of us both writing our names on each other's feet and ankles, it felt so romantic. In our own space, consumed by love and each other.

There was this artistic aspect to the whole experience, of us both exploring our creativity. Learning instruments, writing songs, painting, doing yoga, Qi Gong, Tai Chi, and studying Tantra. It was just a massive explosion of love and exploration of our minds and hearts and each other. We were both pushing the other to grow.

There was so much more I struggled to remember and bring back from the world I was in. There were business ideas, designs, all kinds of stuff. There was a knowing that this was the lifestyle for me: simple. Simple, simplicity and simplify were the words being reverberated around my head; being near family, being near my dad in his final years, looking after him regardless and then doing the same for Fhian's parents, putting our families before all our social commitments.

Of all the places Ayahuasca could have taken me, I was back in Manchester. All the tropical places I've visited over the years, amazing lakes, mountains, coastal towns. It was telling me, 'Chorlton — go there, and friends will follow.' It's got such a rich culture and is close to the city centre that our friends might make the move. Fhian would be happy with what we had, eventually. I just needed to show her.

Other things about past relationships came up, people with attachments to me, things I needed to work on breaking, some unresolved issues. I had been expecting more craziness and visions and journeying into other dimensions. However, I had gotten exactly what I had asked for; clarity of heart and direction.

I sat there in the Buddha position with my head resting on my knee. I was so, so, so happy and smiling. The happiest and most contented smile that had ever graced my face. My whole body was pure love, the pure love of Fhian and Liam, it was intense, and exactly what I'd been waiting for.

Otillia was drawing the ceremony to an end. I had no idea how long it had lasted; time and space had evaporated. She went around each one of us singing her *Icaro's* which she had continued throughout the ceremony. They had provided a beautiful overtone to my sublime visions. Now Otillia was tapping me with this instrument made of dry leaves and singing. A feeling of pure healing ran over my body, tingles passing through every fibre of my being.

It was magical.

The ceremony ended, and I rose to a huge head rush that made me dizzy. I put on my shoes and ventured outside with Dave. I wanted to sit, and process but Dave wanted to talk, so we sat and chatted about our experience in my cabin for about an hour. His experience had been a lot weaker than his previous one with a different Ayahuasquero, but still it had given him a lot of answers to many questions and many ideas.

He worked as a herbalist and had a fascination with the healing powers of tropical plants with an aim to introduce them into mainstream medicine. He was so interesting to talk to and intellectually in another dimension to me, so I just told him about me balls...

I'd remembered another part of my vision was of a house I'd lived in with me mum and me step-dad. The vision showed me my room in that house on Lorna Grove in Gatley and how I used to sit in bed all the time watching TV and playing with my balls like they were stress balls. I relayed this to Dave. I'd spent a good part of the ceremony rekindling my passion for this old trait, obviously with the others unable to see. I wondered why I'd stopped and why I would ever buy stress balls when I had my own impossible-to-lose set constantly at my disposal.

I also got this inclination to send my step-dad an email saying:

Thanks for helping me grow!

Love

Liam

I don't think it meant thanks for letting me grow my passion for playing with my balls as a young lad, but thanks for providing me with the security and discipline I probably needed at the time.

When Dave left, I went outside to look at the stars. Fhian was firmly on my mind, it was like the stars were talking to me. The sky seemed so vast, and millions of stars exploded into my vision, but one star drew my attention. I felt it was trying to tell me something, flashing at me. I focused on it and tried to soak up whatever it was transmitting. Then still feeling pretty high, I crept into my mosquito net covered bed with a picture of Fhian after my heart and mind had spent the whole evening fully entwined with her. I said her name over and over and over and over and over again until I drifted off to the astral plane.

It was my first evening sleeping in the jungle. I felt like I'd been there for so long already as so much had happened. Sleep was difficult, the sound of the jungle was intense, amplified threefold by the cover of darkness. It seemed to bring everything to life, a choir of animal and insect sounds blasting into my dream world. The constant drumming of the cricket, the swamp and river frogs providing the base, birds and amphibians providing a riff, and the monkeys and large animals kicking off the chorus from time to time. Very occasionally, there was a bird that would create this special effect sound that was something like a cross between a foghorn, a kazoo and an ambulance. There were strange rhythmic and often haunting howls, clicks, swishes, buzzes, twitters, swooshes, whirls and whistles. Wilcox again points out that *"the jungle of what one hears is not only the canopy of living things of the jungle but is also the echo of all that humans have been, and we will be. The jungle at night is the sound of memory"*. I lay in wonderment at the sounds I was hearing, the experience I'd just had, the reality of where I was in the world with all the growth and direction I was feeling. I felt clear and very, very happy, something I hadn't felt for a very long time.

I lay wanting daylight. I had no idea of the time, but it seemed like the night was endless. I was looking forward to the morning.

I lay and dreamt about Fhian and our life together.

When I woke, Fhian was there still ever-present in my mind. When daylight came, I got in my hammock and started to write her name on my foot, lots of little Fhian prints starting to form a love heart. I wanted her to see it.

Dave and Ferdinand were both plant medicine doctors. They were working together, searching the jungle for a tree that could cure cancer. I could have done with you two a few years back, I thought. We ate breakfast together and discussed our various travels and work. We all felt the evening's events had been quite mild, but we all seemed to have gotten what we needed from the Ayahuasca and exactly what we'd asked for. It was only Dave's second time, and he said how his first had blown his socks off, shown him all the power of the plants and given him a vast array of visions. I wondered why last night had been so tame in comparison. I asked many questions about the Ayahuasca plant, and about the diet I was on. I had no way of communicating with Otillia and her staff, so it was time for the guys to translate for me. They told me that the two main plants put together to make the brew have various legends and myths as to how they came about. Ayahuasca is said to contain 'The Power and Chacuna', the other main plant is said to contain 'The Light'.

Anthropologists and scholars have for decades been unable to understand how indigenous tribes could have arrived at their extensive knowledge of plant chemistry and healing through trial and error as the complexity of some combinations are equal to anything seen in the west. The people say the plants themselves were the teachers. They say that the preparations for undertaking the journey were given to them by the spirit of the plant itself. After experiencing what I had over the last twelve months, I instinctively knew this to be true. The reality that the plants have spirits like we do and that these spirits can communicate with humans who are switched on to such a frequency makes perfect sense. It seems foreign to the western mind, but who are we to think we know better?

Ayahuasca is fast becoming the psychedelic of choice, and even the FDA (The Food and Drug Administration) in the States approved a study of synthetic DMT (Dimethyltryptamine) which is the main component found in Ayahuasca.

Scientists call it 'The Spirit Molecule'.

It seems that more and more people are rejecting the biology and genetics evolutionary path. They have frustration and disgust with the environmentally destructive, soul-deadening effects of our consumer-driven materialism, which is intense in my own country and impossible to escape in the US. The pop-culture emergence of psychedelics during the 1960s and 70s resulted in a political backlash and the prohibition of LSD and other mind-expanding chemicals. In conjunction with this, I often sat and wondered what the world would be like now if this hard-line hadn't been taken. If hippies hadn't been persecuted? If a balance could have been formed? What would the world be like? I imagine it would be a world that I would have a lot more ease in understanding and being part of.

We all sat around in Otillia's living room for a while. They were all talking Spanish, so I smiled and nodded. I asked what I was to do with my days. Otillia said, "you just rest". We then got talking about the different plants found in the jungle and their healing powers and the specific things they were used for. I started to compile a list, and this is the amazing stuff I was being told:

Guayusa - An aromatic plant whose leaves are commonly used for medical baths. Ayahuasqueros frequently require their patients to bathe with this before a healing session.

Ushpahuasa - A tea made from the plant's roots. It opens your heart chakra to stimulate depth of feeling and help you retrieve memories, especially of childhood. Heals emotions. Traditionally called the rejuvenating plant, it won't erase your wrinkles. It works to loosen the emotional parts and memory. It opens the heart.

Chiric Sanang - Helps move energy through the body.

Sanango - Helps physically disabled people recover their mobility. Even people who have been unable to walk for five years can be cured. They are treated with teas of plants and baths. After two or three months, they can get up and walk again.

Una de Gato - Or Cats Claw, has anti-tumour and anti-inflammatory properties.

Renaco - The rubber tree oozes a white sap that is mixed with alcohol and drunk to cure rheumatism. Healers also apply it directly to joints to ease swelling and pain.

Ochahuaha – The bark is mixed with Ushphausa to make an ointment to treat snakebite.

Yahurapanga – Means "leaf of blood" because it oozes red sap. To treat addiction, especially crack and cocaine addiction. It forces you to vomit, it is very effective. The healer grinds leaves in a food mill and then makes a tea. For prolonged purging, only half a cup is needed. After taking Yahurapanga, addicts are invited to eight sessions of Ayahuasca in eight days, followed by days of Ushpahuasa. That usually takes care of addiction.

Trumpetero or Trumpet Wood – Vegitalistas boil the leaves and stems, and then babies who are on the verge of walking are dipped in the cooled waters. The bath imparts strength to the babies' legs, helping them walk.

Estoraque – A leaf to make tea, this tonic is made to imprint sexual potency to men who are impotent.

Chamburo – Attracts luscious fat worms that the locals fry and eat. Supposed to be delicious and provides protein and rich oils.

Bobinsana – Does not fall down as its roots are so deep. Ingested, it makes a person more connected to nature and as the root of the plant opens up, so does the person.

Chuchuhuasi – Is tall with a big trunk. It gives endurance to the body.

Juster Sacha – A relatively rare creeper vine with distinctive heart-shaped leaves that are boiled to make a tea. This must be left overnight to be exposed to dew. Only then is it ready to treat kidney problems.

It was mental to think about the vast plethora of medicines that were at the disposal of those living in the Amazon. What gifts nature has to offer our children and us, but in the west we know so little about the healing powers of plants. More often than not big businesses exploit them, coming in and destroying land and contaminating the spirit of the plants.

After the amazing revelations of what the Amazon had to offer, it was time for the guys to leave. They were off deeper into the jungle in search of their super cancer plant.

I wished them well.

When they left, the realisation dawned on me that I was unable to communicate again. After my next encounter with Ajo Sacha, all I wanted to do was relax in my hammock. Ferdinand had told me that Ajo Sacha was given to relieve body pain and allow my mind to be clear. I thought I'd just been tired when I first arrived and lay in the hammock all day, dozing, listening, thinking, not thinking, watching. After that day's dose, I did the same. I couldn't remember the last time I'd just sat and done nothing, no reading, no writing, no music, no conversation, no other people. I was in no way bored, and it was joyful and refreshing to be doing nothing with no pressure to be achieving anything. I actually felt I was achieving so much by just being.

This was what I did the whole day until I went to get water. I was then asked by Otillia if I wanted to do a ceremony again that evening.

"*Si bien,*" I said, basking in the glory of the fluidity of my Spanish.

Again I didn't feel prepared, but soon I was called for another flower bath, taking my time to soak. I spotted another guy walking about, a westerner, not one of Otillia's staff. I assumed others would be joining in tonight and without any evening meal, I was called to the ceremonial space.

CHAPTER 2
THE TERROR

The setting was exactly the same; three rolled mattresses laid out against the wooden plank walls. A tall, slender gentleman sat in the spot Dave had occupied the previous evening. Being typically English, I went for the same seat I'd had last night.

The new guy and Otillia were chatting in Spanish. I smile and nod, feeling a bit nervous and useless. The guy came over to introduce himself. He was called Ollie.

I felt like I'd had a little more time to prepare for the ceremony. I knew I wanted a stronger journey, to see more visuals, and visions and to be taken far, far away. A lady then joined the room, and again the tradition began. This time a darker looking liquid was produced from a bag in a two-litre plastic bottle. The prayers and blessings were said, and we were all blown with smoke. Ollie was first to drink, and I remember thinking my stomach didn't feel as strong as it had the previous night.

Was this due to it being emptier because of the fasting or was it a bit dodgy?

I was then called up and given my brew. It seemed thicker and darker and more pungent than the previous evening. I held up the cup, blew on it three times, setting my intentions, "to be able to see" and, "for my mind to be cleared". I knocked back the liquid, it tasted so much worse. Was it the same brew, I thought? Or was it because I was feeling different? Instantly on returning to my mat, I was finding it hard to keep down. Was this punishment for my uncontrollable ego last night? I sat trying to get comfortable, hoping beyond hope to keep the liquid down. It seemed to be bubbling in the top of my throat, and I battled to keep it at bay. The lady then drank her brew, then Otillia and the candle was blown out.

I was starting to sweat, praying it would stay down, my mouth constantly filling up with liquid bile, which as soon as I'd swallowed it, was back in my mouth which led to several minutes of discomfort and frustration.

I was really fighting the sensation to not be sick.

I looked around, determined not to be the first to spew. Everyone else seemed to be comfortable, it was going to be me, I knew it. I was really struggling, but all of a sudden, an air of calm engulfed me, my body settled, and I felt normal again. Visuals began and again they were in black and white but more multi-dimensional, then the battle began again, and my mouth was full of liquid. I was determined not to let it out, frightful that I would not get its full effects with it being in my body for such a short period. I had thoughts of a story I'd heard about a guy going clubbing, who would take a pill and be sick when it started to take effect. He would then root around in the sick to find the pill and take it again. There was no way I was eating my sick!

'Hold it down, Browne,' I kept telling myself. 'If it comes out, you're not eating your sick.' The liquid came, and I swallowed, and after another few minutes I felt I had control again and sat back and relaxed. Then I felt the depth of my stomach explode, and everything came racing up. I reached for my bucket and spewed, my guts hitting the bowl just as my arms brought it into the line of fire.

I felt defeated, first to blow. Was this punishment for my ego? Would I now see nothing? Was the ceremony going to be pointless for me? Had I lost my latest opportunity to travel with Lady Ayahuasca?

I had no idea that what was about to unfold would change me forever.

The purging was violent. Four times the depths of my stomach were emptied. Then as I wiped my mouth of the disgusting residue, I closed my eyes to be welcomed into another world. Fluttering geometric patterns, morphing into figures, jungle sounds which I can only describe as the alien sounds from movies like *Predator* and *District 9* fluttered into my ears. I saw beautiful otherworldly creatures similar to those from *Avatar*, but with Egyptian-style longer heads and headdresses that were not headdresses but their actual heads. They looked a bit like the Williams sisters when they'd first hit the news with their beaded hair, but an alien version. I was shown visual perfection only for it to be replaced by a greater visual perfection, which made the previous seem trivial, old and unimaginative. I opened my eyes and visions from within were imprinting onto the world.

I decided to lie down and enjoy, a decision I have now discovered is never advised. It is said it can invoke the darker side of Ayahuasca. Lady Ayahuasca demands respect for you to remain upright and focused. I read this a day or two later, so there and then I just sank into my mattress in pure bliss, unaware of the danger that lay ahead. My knees were up and my back completely flat on the floor, placing each vertebra individually on to the wood, my hands crossed onto my chest. My eyes were closed, and I was in Heaven. It was Paradise, but a million times better than I could have ever imagined. There were shapes I had never seen before, vibrating and pulsating colours, fluttering figures flickering into view. This was more like what I'd been expecting.

I was fully submerged in another world.

These complex beings with their braided headdresses, were less human than the aliens in *Avatar*, more elaborate, with huge eyes and elegantly sculpted faces, they were like sophisticated robots, ones you could imagine existing in a few hundred years.

My inner world was illuminated.

I was shocked by its vastness, the infinity of shapes and colours that had erupted in my mind. Time and space seemed to stand still. The present didn't exist, and neither did the future and the past, but at the same time, they all existed simultaneously in each different realm. I started to stretch out and loosen my body, moving the sick bowl to one side with my foot and the blissful feeling of my limbs fully extended and stretching erupted up my body and into my head, this electric current fizzing all around my scalp. I stretched out my arms, moving the drinking water to the side, my body reaching as far as it could and my mind starting to do the same. I was seeing, this was it, this is what I'd asked for. I was yawning a lot, big deep yawns that brought me bliss and satisfaction, my body feeling like it was reaching its full potential, half on the mattress half on the wooden floor, I was parallel with the wall now.

Bliss and love-filled me. Fhian and my baby were back, and I held them so close, so tight, knowing this was all that mattered. I could feel the presence of my mum, of her approval and her deep love. It literally blew away any love I had ever felt before. More intense, meaningful and beautiful than any love that had ever existed. That was my family right there, the security and stability I'd been looking for, I'd created it, I held on and held on. Bliss engulfed me, and I felt like I would explode with pure abundant love all over everybody's faces.

I was now upside down, my legs were up the wooden wall, I wanted to be upside down, to turn the world on its head. My head and shoulders stayed on the ground, but my feet insisted on being the highest part of my body. They were stretching and tapping, flinging themselves about. I really wanted to be upside down, maybe it was because I was in the Southern Hemisphere and at home that would mean I was the right way up?

It was the first time in a while I felt like I could stretch unbridled. My body had been so tense, and sore and I hadn't known why. The plant diet had made me so tired the last two days that time in my hammock was all that had mattered.

I went into a shoulder stand.

I couldn't help it, my body just did it. I hoped it didn't seem like I was showing off.

I hadn't moved for five hours the previous night, and here I was all over the place. I then went into a wheelbarrow and a crab. I utterly had no control, this was all just happening and my body felt so good. I felt free with it, but the real me would have been petrified at the spectacle I was making of myself. My upright limbs crashed down with a thud, then I clasped my feet and stretched my leg out fully. All the while, visual after visual cascaded my inner eye and I watched as my head whirled around in blissful glee. I was tapping and banging and making sounds with my mouth, like an institutionalised loon.

Otillia's beautiful *Icaro* began, and this transported me to another level further, it was like the music was a spaceship, and she was the driver, and we went off into the Universe. My body reacted further to the music, tapping, banging, smashing and crashing. My floating arms would crash around from side to side like a monkey.

When the music stopped, I became instantly still, frozen. I would become aware of my body, and it was always stuck in the weirdest positions. I observed myself with my limbs piled on top of me but finding it so, so comfortable.

I then started to play with gravity, holding my limbs up high and then, as if gravity had been turned up really high, I would release the limb, and it would hurtle towards the Earth and crash down onto my chest or face, and I would make a crash sound with my mouth to add effect. I briefly turned my head to the other drinkers, they were sat completely still like sedated chimps in a zoo. I gazed in amazement while my tongue whirled around my mouth frantically. I had no control at all, then the music stopped, and I stayed completely still for what seemed like an eternity. It was as if the whole atmosphere of the world was collapsing on me. Pinned to the floor by an imaginary large piece of glass, I lay holding it like some horizontal French mime artist. I was so still, worried I would never be released. Gravity had been turned up so high, and I was being pinned down to the wooden floor. The next thing I know I was tucked around my mattress, holding it tight, resting my head on it mumbling, "Mamma, Mamma," wanting her near. My eyes were enquiring, and I could see the moon through a gap in the wooden walls. Wow, it's so bright and beautiful, I thought, with perfect ribbons of clouds drifting by it, giving it a real cinematic feel. I studiously lined it up, so it was perfectly in the middle of the gap between the wooden slats. I gawped at its beauty as if right now the moon and the sky were only for me.

People and their jobs went through my mind, the way society was festering in me, our continual race to meet expectations, the jobs we do, their meaning, their greater good. I wanted to drag Fhian away, take us away, take us home. Away from the swarm of society that wouldn't let go of its perceptions, illusions and patterns of behaviour that it holds onto so tightly in fear of anything different, being brainwashed enough to die for what it thinks it believes in.

Nothing seemed real.

The number of pointless jobs, people building, destroying, suffering, hating, shitting and dying! Just to occupy themselves and ensure they don't look within. I started to laugh, laugh so hard at what so many people did with their time, how serious they took their roles, how little fun they had and most of the time at a detriment to the environment, Mother Earth and their own personal health. I couldn't stop laughing, it wasn't at people, it was at the madness of the system. Deep, guttural laughs echoed around the room. Then I snapped myself out of it.

Otillia's *Icaro* began, and I meandered back through space and time. I was being taken on a magical mystery tour. Gravity was occasionally turned up, and I was starting to feel stuck, starting to have difficulty with reality and how gravity actually worked. Confusion engulfed me, my limbs would tap, noises would spill from my mouth, and I had no control and no idea what was real. The music stopped, and I froze, every muscle in my body tensed and then I let everything crash down to the floor, and I lay silently for a moment, manoeuvring beautifully with my limbs as the music ended in my mind.

I was then flung back into confusion. What was my hand? What were my ideas? What was life? Is this my leg? Who are you? Does anything matter? Why was I born there? Why has life been hard? Is this a room? I sat there curled up and confused, shaking a little. I felt abused, it was like I was being poked at, my skin being pulled. I was being raped, jabbed, my eyes torn out, fingered, my penis torn off, abused. It was this confirmation that we were moving into the age of the feminine, and it was time for me to pay for the male condition. *It's your turn, it's your turn to suffer now* was going through my head and I felt disgusted by the way women had always been treated. I could feel their pain, all their misery, all their despair. I was taking it all on, I was suffering for all the times I had taken women for granted, seeing them as objects for so long.

I lay there in my own mess, shit, piss, sick, sweat and vomit all covered me, I had no idea if it was real. I felt stuck, trapped, unable to move my body. None of my limbs felt like mine. I realised that I am not my body, whatever happens to it is irrelevant, it's the soul that counts, your soul can endure any physical damage to the body.

I was being told that abuse of any sort can be healed, repaired, fixed, and my body became a worthless piece of flesh.

I sprang up, grabbed my sick bucket and on all fours, forcefully erupted once again.

From deep down it rose up through me, splattering into the bowl. Every time I wretched it was as if part of me was disappearing, all the dogma from parents, society, government, marketing, religion and consumerism. All the pain that had been inflicted on me as a child was coming out. Everything I had no choice about was being stripped away from my soul.

My soul wanted me clean, wanted me healed, wanted me to see the light, to see the truth, to follow my truth. It wanted me to rid myself of this baggage, these wounds, the anger, the pain and the suffering, so as not to pass it on to my children.

I had to learn from my parents' mistakes, not repeat them. I was being cleansed, ridded of this anguish, putting myself through this for the greater good. I was going back to where I was when I entered this world as a child, an empty vessel, without illusions, beliefs, opinions and prejudices. We become infected as we grow, and I no longer had to carry around the baggage I didn't want and did not choose. I crashed back down, feeling light, feeling like nothing mattered any more. Sweat was dripping from every one of my pores. I was drenched, so hot, grabbing at my clothes to allow some air in.

I took in the moon again and found some comfort as if it was home.

Then I started to feel more and more trapped, my concept of time redundant, occasionally hearing or seeing Otillia captaining the spacecraft. I was here in this room, and I became a monkey fascinated again with my hands and feet, climbing the wall, shitting and pissing freely from trees, primordial instincts filled me. I started to feel more and more empty and more and more lost, only very occasionally getting a thought. I felt stuck in this animal's body, rocking from side to side and forwards and backwards on my back, as my fingers hooked themselves around my toes and I experimented with the flexibility of my body parts.

Next, I was slithering around the floor, I was a snake now pinned to the ground on my back and belly, making hissing noises as opposed to monkey ones. I think it was at this point Ollie approached me and asked if I could stop the noises and the banging. Spaced out and looking at him upside down, I said, "I can't help it, man, I have no control," and went happily back to being a snake. The sound of everything amplified. I could hear the jungle with superhero hearing, and every time a fly or mosquito came near me, I flicked out my tongue to capture it. My eyes flicked from side to side, focusing intently on my prey. Again I found myself trapped against the floor, my head, shoulders and arms pinned by this huge invisible object that was on top of me.

I became some creature that lived under the water's surface. I would snatch my hands up when insects passed so I could feed. It was damp and soggy, I was sure I had been trapped in this amphibian's body for many years, life afterlife. Then past lives were flashing through my mind, not mine exactly but the concept. It felt like this was another life, my soul, the 'I' that knew my consciousness was in this amphibian's body. I was living this life in the body of a small amphibian but with my awareness and consciousness still intact. I was enduring this hellish nightmare as punishment for a lesson I hadn't learnt and the bad lives I'd previously lived. Little snippets of information seemed to prick my brain, life was being assessed in a scary way, its point, its meaning on the bigger scale. It seemed inconsequential and meaningless. But then when I looked at it on the scale of the world, our solar system, the galaxies and the universe and all the other universes, it was so very, very insignificant. Less significant than us on this planet, cutting a piece of sand for a million years and saying that final grain we had, had any significance. It had no significance, but at the same time is as significant as everything else, because it is everything else. Still, you would never get to a more insignificant piece on the larger scale of our individual lives in comparison to all that is, but still, we are part of all that is.

I then started to doubt my life. Was it real? Was this my life right here on the floor in this hut or under the water as the amphibian?

Had I imagined the life I'd lived?

I started to firmly believe that everyone I'd ever met, every experience I'd ever had, was conceived in my imagination from where I now lay. I was so unsure, so many moments of my life flashed before my eyes. Were they real? Had I imagined them? Were all the people actors, was I in some kind of *Truman Show*? I felt like I may have created my own life in my own mind. I'd made it all up, everything that had taken place, every event, every person. It had all been a fragment of my imagination. I was saddened by the reality I'd created and the fact it had only existed in my head. I began to accept that all of the people close to me had never existed, I'd imagined them and created them out of boredom whilst waiting for a bug to feed on as I lay under the water's surface. My core knew that everything was an illusion, an illusion within an illusion, within a dream. I had no idea of what was real and what was not and what exactly those two things meant. I seemed to be trapped in a paradox that my brain could not fathom and all I could do was drool. I could make no sense of reality, I was here, I was stuck. I felt like Brad Pitt in 12 *Monkeys* or Jack Nicholson at the end of *One Flew Over the Cuckoo's Nest*. I had completely lost it. I drooled and without any control watched my limbs, urging them to move, but they would not. I drifted from my old reality to my new, shame-filled me. I had been trapped in the Ayahuasca institution for either 16, 1000 or an infinite number of years. There were no other numbers.

It was definitely one of these amounts of time.

That was so clear to me.

I'd let my family down with my life and my actions.

I imagined my mum's sorrow for her only son wallowing away in his own madness, unable to control any of his bodily functions. I was hearing all my friends and acquaintances gossiping about how they knew I would lose the plot a long time ago. "If anyone would lose it, you could put money on it being Liam," I heard.

Internally I screamed, 'noooooooooooooooooooooo,' ripping at my own body, annoyed with what had become of me. I was never going to fulfil any of my dreams, my own family, watching my babies grow, my only want in life had now disappeared forever, never to be fulfilled, lost, redundant and I was stuck here for the rest of time. Like Bill Murray in *Groundhog Day*, I was on a loop, and I was unable to escape. I was so scared, petrified even that everything was ruined, and I was a failure. I'd gone a step too far in my pursuit of freedom, of wisdom, of enlightenment and now I was just covered in piss and shit.

I looked around the room I'd been stuck in all this time; 16, 1000 or an infinite number of years. The other two people who had started the ceremony were long gone. I was there alone, being abused by my own mind under the watchful eye of Otillia. She had been keeping watch of me all this time since my incident, since I became lost from reality, since I'd been unable to function in the real world.

Or was this the real world, had everything been made up? Doubts and fears of everything pursued my thoughts. I was wrangling with this fine line of what anything was and what anything had ever been.

It was frightening to be in a position of not believing anything that went through your mind, being unable to summon your body to do anything you wanted it to do. This must be how some disabled and mentally handicapped people feel, and I was truly experiencing it. I firmly believed this was my life from now on; a constant battle, a constant struggle, unable to do anything for myself.

The open door then came into focus. Maybe one day soon I could summon enough energy to get out of that door. Maybe then I could lift myself from this mess and make it outside and then to my hut. I lay contemplating this for another eternity with as much concentration as a prison break. Finally, after more internal wars, battles and disagreements, I mustered the courage and energy to lift myself.

I staggered to the door, the blood instantaneously rushing to my head like a waterfall barraging and churning the depths of the water below. This turned off the lights of my mind, and I thought I'd lost my chance and any second guards would rush in, putting me into a straitjacket and bundling me into an isolation chamber.

As the lights of my eyes re-established the world around them, I focused again on leaving this *Apocalypse Now* style prisoner of war camp for the insane.

As I peered at what had been my surrounding for the last 16, 1000 or an infinite number of years, the moonstruck a series of beautiful white lines across the floor of the darkened hut as it broke through the gaps in the wooden wall. The light was now fully returned to my eyes. I balanced at the top of the steps leading down from the room to the jungle floor. With all the energy and concentration I could muster, I navigated the darkened, wooden steps to freedom.

I was out.

I rushed towards my hut through the gardens like a prisoner to freedom, and like a prisoner I panicked about what awaited me on the outside. This realisation stopped me in my tracks, and I stood frozen, my body stuck, my mind stuck. Was there even a hut?

Was I heading the right way if there was one?

Would I end up walking deep into the jungle and be lost forever, eaten alive by its inhabitants?

Where was I?

Was this a dream?

Finally, I came to the conclusion I was stuck in *Groundhog Day*. I was not Bill Murray, I was Liam Browne, I was trapped in a day for all of time. I knew this exact situation, I had been here before, that much was clear. I felt that safety was back in Otillia's room. But I didn't want that safety, I needed out of that torture, out of that worse-than-Hell situation. I knew I had to go forward, hut or no hut. I walked and started to think I was seeing the same things over and over again, trees, landscapes, over and over I passed the same repeated sequence, over and over as I trod barefoot, slugging through shallow pools of snakes which had now become the ground. I could feel them slithering smoothly between my toes and twisting and constricting themselves around my ankles. Every time I lifted my leg, I would have to shake them off.

One tall tree stood out just ahead.

I recognised that tree.

I decided to remember it and make sure I passed it.

I tied a mental piece of string to that tree. But I just kept passing it and passing it, thousands of times. The sequence was on loop, and I started to panic again. I kept being flung back to where I had started.

Finally, I got past it, and in the distance my hut appeared. I ran for it, shaking snakes from my feet. Safety beckoned. I was free, then, as I was running, I questioned whether it was my hut.

Had I ever been there before?

Was there ever a hut?

Who was waiting for me in there?

I decided death was better than the eternity I'd just spent trapped on the floor.

When I finally got into the hut, nothing seemed real, objects would warp coming towards me and then bend the other way. I felt like I had been lured here, it was a trick. I'd fallen into a trap. I quickly needed safety, and the only place that offered any was my bed protected by the impenetrable force that was my mosquito net. I crawled under the net, tucked it back under the mattress and lay in a foetal position facing the wall.

Sweating, damp and dirty, I was unable to understand anything.

How long had I been gone?

Was I safe now?

What was going on?

This is where they had wanted me, I thought. In my straitjacket, trapped in this little space, I was now stuck here. I screamed in my head, not wanting anyone to hear. I lay petrified, curled up as tight as I could. I felt like a baby, not a man. I thought of Fhian and never seeing her again. Disgust at what I had done filled me. I'd let my mind take over, I'd been tricked, made to look a fool, there was nothing I could do. Dread engulfed my whole pathetic body and self. I lay for hour upon hour, and then someone was in my room.

I heard them enter.

I stayed perfectly still, trying not to breathe. Was this it? Was I about to die? Things were crashing around, footsteps slowly stepped on the floorboards which creaked in an eerie fashion. I was too scared to move, to speak, to do anything. I was praying I would be safe, hoping they would not kill me. I wanted them to just take what they wanted and leave. I was listening in that scared way, where your breathing becomes so shallow you can't hear it and you hold your breath for as long as possible for optimum sound intake. I listened and listened. The person moved around and then took a long piss in my toilet. I wondered who it was. Why hadn't I shut the door on my way in?

Even if I had, there was no lock, and the walls were made of wood, and the windows had no glass in them.

I was unable to do anything with my body. It was so tense and contorted. I was trapped, confused, petrified, and I was now having to deal with a madman pissing in my toilet. His footsteps moved around after he finished and shook, my ears following his every move. He turned into my room, he approached my bed. I could feel him just on the other side of my mosquito net. What was he going to do? I could hear and feel his breath. Who was he? What did he want? Please make it fast, I thought.

I wanted to turn and look so badly, just to get a glimpse, but I was frozen. I hadn't moved a muscle for so long now, and my last breath seemed minutes and minutes ago. I was playing dead and remained as still as humanly possible. My inspiration was one of those guys in the city who paints himself metallic grey and stands like a statue for hours. Only I didn't want money, I just wanted this guy gone. It was such male energy, I could still feel and hear his guttural breathing, in and out. He felt so close he must have been staring at me as I could sense no other movement. An eternity passed, and I drifted in and out of consciousness. The breathing had finally stopped.

I lay there, and my next sensory stimulation started to come from straight in front of me, just on the other side of the wooden wall that my nose was almost touching. Still, I hadn't moved, God only knows how long I had been frozen for.

Soft music began to play. I recognised it as an *Icaro*, hearing the flowing sounds accompanied by the rattle of the dried leaves. It was like Otillia was outside my room, healing me, bringing me back to some level of normality, performing this ritual to close off the ceremony, to avoid bad energies entering me, closing me to outside interference.

I felt a glow return to my face, felt the heaviness leave my body. It was beautiful and magical to just listen, but again it messed up me head. What was real here? Was I imagining all this or had Otillia come to sing close to my bed to heal me? I had no idea. I was again still trapped and petrified, unable to grasp the real and unreal. However, with every sound and shake of the leaves, my mood continued to lighten. After some time of happily listening to these soothing beats, some sort of reality started to return. All I could think about was going home, not wanting to be insane anymore or risk insanity further by staying.

I finally got up, used the toilet and on the way back to my bed, grabbed my picture of Fhian. I just lay there looking at my beautiful goddess, deciding I couldn't risk never seeing her again and never having babies with her. Tomorrow, as soon as the sun came up, I would pack and leave and get back to my sweetheart as soon as possible.

It seemed like morning would never come again. The rooster under my bed gave me the premature expectation of daylight with his, 'cockadoodledo'-ing on three separate occasions. Or was this another thing I was imagining?

Daylight finally arrived.

I was still set on leaving.

I wanted to talk to Otillia first and tell her my decision.

What had happened to me?

Was it normal?

Breakfast was called, and Ollie and Guylene were already in the commodore. I apologised for my noise and constant movement. They said what I had done was pretty funny and very entertaining but at the same time disturbed them from their own experience. They then told me how I'd left the ceremony early.

I said, "No, you were gone when I left".

They said, "No, you left after only two hours, not even halfway through."

"Noooooooooo that can't be, I was there for so, so long."

"No," they concurred, "you left quickly and didn't return".

I'd only been in the room two hours? It seemed absurd, but it had to be true. They were both a lot more sound of mind than I was. I wondered how so many lifetimes of events could have taken place in only a couple of hours. I truly thought I'd died and been trapped there for eternity, but eternity was only two hours in this reality? I was astounded and shocked.

I pondered on reality; was that my reality, is this my reality, what is reality, was that my future reality? Reality seemed such a personal thing, two people can see the exact same event, but their reality of it is completely different. It all depends on where they are coming from and where they're going and what else is on their mind at the time. We all see things differently, and we have to accept that everyone else sees it differently to us and remember not to push our own reality on others too much. There is a Cesar Calvo quote that sums this up quite nicely, *"Things are not truly real, or only mere illusions. There are many categories in between, where things exist, many categories of the real, simultaneously and in different times"*.

Ollie had been travelling for a few months, and this was the fourth time he had done Ayahuasca. He was a tall, fair-haired, spectacled Swedish young man and Guylene was a fifty-something French lady with short grey hair, a tooth-filled smile that lit up the room and infected all around her with the happiness her expression created. She was a filmmaker living in Paris, and she interviewed myself and Ollie as I was still engulfed in fear, fascination and frustration.

Ollie's Spanish was excellent, and he agreed to translate what I wanted to ask Otillia and soon we all sat in the ceremonial room discussing the night's events. Ollie and Guylene's Spanish had reiterated how non-existent my own was. Fear, ever-present self-doubt and disappointment circled my mind. Did I not have an ear for languages, or was I just lazy? Was it another thing I wanted to do but wouldn't put the hard work into? I pondered...

I asked Otillia if what had happened to me was normal.

She said, "It can happen, part of your true self came out, but you were filled with fear. You need this diet and this time to learn and grow. Last night's brew was strong with the Ayahuasca still in your system from the previous night, but your fear more than anything stepped forward, and that is what you have to overcome. Not being scared of who you truly are, stepping out of the costume of values and ego you've had people dressing you up with all your life. You need to step out of that and claim your power as yours. Step forward as the true you. The plants will help you overcome this and teach you who you are. It is a lesson you have to make sacrifices for. With the diet, the restrictions, and allowing your mind and heart to be directed, your body, soul and spirit will be healed."

I told her that I had thought of leaving that day, flying home to my girl and asking her to marry me and that I wanted that commitment to have her as my family and then to have babies. She laughed and said, "You can't go back as you are, you behaved like a child, unable to control your actions, allowing your body and mind to be lost and unable to redeem your power. Who wants to marry that? Fathers have to be strong. We will get you there this week, these plants will take form in you and do this work, you need to see out the week and finish what you have started. Set your intentions in the next ceremony, but until then just take the plants and be still."

She would be trying other plants on me to try and lower my fear, give me strength and be mentally ready for the next ceremony and the next chapter in my life. We laughed about my monkey movements and shortly after regaining my faith in staying for the rest of the week, Guylene and Ollie left, and it was back to my language-less world.

The next four days were very solitary. I spent all my time in my hut, dividing it between the bed and hammock, occasionally reading and writing. It was paradise for me. I would wake up, get in the hammock, be called for breakfast, drink some tea and my Ajo Sacha, return to the hammock, doze, maybe write, think about Fhian and missing my family and friends.

Some days I would be called for lunch, some days not, and I would wait till tea time. A flower bath could happen at any time. All of my other time was spent in my room. There were too many bugs and insects to sit out on the grass, and it was so damp and humid that the hammock was the perfect escape from everything.

I'd had no idea of time since I'd arrived. Otillia did have a clock in the main room, but it always said 10:50 and every day I would forget it didn't work, assuming breakfast had been called late. I now also had no idea of the day or date, but I didn't need to know any of this. Here now, none of it mattered, and I imagined all the billions of people in cities all over the world running around to a tight schedule. Someone would come and tell me if it was time for food or a bath, saying, "*Señor, banyo*" or "*Señor, desyanuno*". It was amazing to not have to think about anything, not once was I bored or agitated. I just sat peacefully, swinging in my hammock, hour after hour, taking naps, having very little energy and absolutely no desire to do anything else. This must have been due to the plants and the diet. Usually I would be doing yoga, or press-ups and sit-ups, exploring my surroundings but never once did I feel like any of that. Before I arrived, I'd thought that with all the free time I would get myself super fit, but no, it was just hammock relaxation time for now.

The heavens would open, and torrential rain would fall. I would watch the droplets bounce almost a foot above the ground, and I would listen to the drops opening fire on my tin roof as damp moisture filled the air and the mosquitoes surrounded the net around my bed, waiting for an opening to get to my tasty flesh.

Darkness would arrive, and on the four nights, there were no ceremonies I went to bed shortly after sunset. The sky became completely black, and I could see nothing. I'd run out of candles on the second night, so the only option was to go to sleep early. I was actually the only person travelling or just living in these parts that did not have a torch. It was so magical to be at the mercy of nature and to be living by its true ways.

I lay listening. It was a challenge to try and decipher what it was exactly making each noise. I found the bird noises the most soothing, there was one that sounded like a laser being shot. There was one like a crazy mobile ringtone, one like the ping-pong before an announcement in a public place and lots of sirens and further pongs.

One night I heard monkeys fighting. It was like war had broken out around my hut. I wish I could have seen what was taking place and known what the disagreement was about. The crickets and insects provided a steady backing track to any other action taking place.

One the fifth or sixth morning I was brought my Ajo Sacha. As I downed it I realised it wasn't Ajo Sacha, it was something else. Otillia's assistant said "*plantas*", which is the word for all plants. I thought, well I can't ask what it is because I don't know how to, so I just waited to see what happened. Without moving from the hammock which swung close to the door, I watched the curvy lady, whose clothes were dirty and wet from the damp heat return to the main house. I then got back to looking into space and rocking.

Within five minutes, parts of my body started to tingle. It was like a liquid, or energy was making its way through my bloodstream, entering every fibre of me, all my organs, vessels, cells and the hairs all over me stood on end. As it circulated through my veins, each part of my body it passed would start to vibrate and tingle. It was like someone had tipped a full bottle of energising body wash all over me, but more intense and not just on the outside but deep within me. I felt a little dizzy and spun out, but vitalised and present.

On the day of my final ceremony, I was called to breakfast. I'd noticed how this was the first day I'd felt a little agitated like I had some energy and needed to be active. The heat had intensified and the rain which had been on and off the whole week hadn't stopped since the previous night. It was like someone was dropping swimming pools onto my tin roof. The mosquitoes had gone from a few here and there to an infestation in my damp, hot hut. I couldn't hammock without a constant battle with that evil taunt of the mosquito buzz. For hours I slapped and banged my legs, feet, arms and chest, trying to kill what seemed my only enemy in this world. My only safety seemed to be my bed and net, and now with the sheer numbers I couldn't even get in there without a few stowaways cadging a lift on some part of my body as I wriggled under. They would have to be decimated before I could relax and rest. Endless minutes were spent identifying my targets and going in for the kill, often to find that when my mission had been successful I would have blood on my hands from this piece of pure evil that had already taken part of me, making revenge feel all the sweeter.

Later that day, I decided to venture to the hut next to mine. It was a good twenty metres away, and I'd never had the desire to go and have a look before, being so very happy with all that I had in my hut. It was identical to my own. I found a full box of candles and thought if I'd made this arduous journey a few days earlier I could have had light after sunset.

As I made my way back to my hut, exhausted after this new and challenging adventure, a white couple came towards me. As soon as I started to talk, I felt a bit spaced out, the new medicine had been pretty intense. The couple were Lucias and Lisa, and they were from Oregon. I was particularly struck by how good-looking they were. He had these intense blue eyes, and the green of her eyes really drew me to them until I discovered her very large breasts. I wasn't sure if it was me or them on another planet. They had this air of higher consciousness about them and seemed to be floating. Everything was melting into everything else, and I was identifying more with the way I was feeling in the presence of other people. I discovered I would be in ceremony with them later that evening.

Lucias had first seen Otillia four years ago, with the rough directions of getting off a bus at Kilometre 51 *en route* from Iquitos to Nakula and walk into the jungle for 30 minutes until you reach a hut. He said his life had changed from that moment on. He felt he'd found his path and had been to see Otillia every year since. They were now both energy healers back in Oregon and spiritual work, including music, dance and travel seemed to be their thing.

I felt a bit jealous. They really impressed me, I wanted part of what they had. Their lives seemed perfect, living in the beautiful countryside, with beautiful each other, so happy, so comfortable in their skin and sure of their path. I told them about the crazy experience I'd had four days before, and they advised me to stay sat upright, make clear my intentions, not leaving them open to interpretation, so they are not taken literally.

Ayahuasca had done exactly what I'd asked for, shown me what it could do and shown me how it would feel to lose my mind. Something I wasn't in a rush to experience again, and so I was considering what it was I wanted from this ceremony; my soul's path to be shown to me and the way I was to follow it. I wanted to connect to my higher self and figure out what I was on this Earth to do.

What was God's plan for me?

How could I follow that and be shown a path?

What parts of my life should I concentrate on?

I felt I had so many interests, so many things I enjoyed and felt passionate about, but was unable to commit to any of them as I always felt like I had so much going on. I was never settled, never in one place and felt this anxious dissatisfaction continuously. I really wanted to feel rooted, to have family and good friends and a community around me. I wanted to be in one place, create a home, a base, somewhere I could up and leave, go and work on disaster relief or eco-house building projects, but know I always had that home to come back to.

My main intention for that evening was to be able to control the experience to an extent, not be as lost as last time. I decided to go with "please show me my life's purpose and give me some direction."

With that imprinted, I was really looking forward to the ceremony. I felt blessed to have Lucias there to translate again, lucking out by having bilingual people at each ceremony to tell me what Otillia was saying and to be able to pass on my questions the following morning. I had felt blessed, so often on this trip, everything had just seemed to fall into place. The less I worried, the more everything I needed and wanted was provided for me. Maybe it was my new faith in that being the best way to live my life, maybe it was all the amazing trinkets and crystals I had been given by people I love back home and the way this energy was looking out for me, or maybe it was all the work I was doing in meditation, yoga and continually looking for growth and ways to improve myself. Whatever it was, I loved it, and it made life a breeze when it happened. Every time I meditated or prayed or intensely focused on something, it was provided, arrived or happened. If I only knew what to ask for, what exactly I wanted, then I could just focus on that and get it.

A deep hunger started to fill me. I hadn't felt hungry the whole week. I knew I had to fast as it was the day of the ceremony, but with the heat, the humidity, the moisture and the mosquitoes I was massively agitated.

The light of the sun went out. The black blanket covered with stars was pulled over my head and hut. Time was now ticking down until the ceremony. I felt the nervous anticipation I would feel prior to playing in a Cup Final, excitement and fear brewing together. I washed myself, throwing bowls of water over my head, feeling it caress every part of me before hitting the wooden floor and escaping through the cracks onto the jungle bed below. I got dressed, covering as much skin as possible so as not to allow the continual mosquito biting. I waited to be called, rocking from side to side in the hammock, trying to keep a good speed so no mosquitoes could settle.

The mosquitos got too much, so I stood outside under the stars, waiting. I couldn't handle them, they were on me, so I went to the safety of my bed. Time was passing, it wasn't usually this long after it went dark that I was called for ceremony.

I waited and waited, but no one came.

I tried to relax, but nothing stilled my mind. I thought maybe Otillia wasn't going to have me there due to my behaviour in the last ceremony. I thought I heard music.

Had they started without me?

Would that happen?

I tried to steady my mind and drift off to sleep, convincing myself that whatever happened was exactly what should happen. I tried to clear my mind totally, make it as clear as it had been the previous days. Was it the fact I hadn't had my Ajo Sacha today? My mind leapt off, making conclusions and theories, I wanted out of it and to relax, not to worry and to feel peaceful again.

"*Señor, señor*" was being called from my door just as I'd drifted off.

"*Si, si*", I said and jumped out of my bed and net. I collected my candle, water jug and shoes and headed for what all my travels had been pointing towards; hoping Ayahuasca would re-cognate my mind, lead me to my heart and soul's desires. I wanted to be free of my own expectations of myself, be free of society's expectations of me, free of the dogma that continually builds up Lemming-like attributes that take us away from our true selves. I wanted to be who I should be, know the inner workings of who I am and know my heart and its convictions, to prepare me for a beautiful life of love, family, friendship, health and happiness. I wanted to explore more of the creative side that had been shown to me in my first session, I wanted more guidance. I felt I'd underachieved in the acting world due to my lack of confidence and inability to fully go for it, which mirrored my inability to fully commit to anything.

I made my way to the ceremony room, plodding along on the same route I had navigated a few nights previous which then had seemed endless and covered in snakes.

Otillia was in her usual spot. Lucias was to her left and Lisa took the seat I'd been in the previous two ceremonies. I took the one directly facing Otillia.

Guylene was there, not to drink this evening, but to record Otillia's *Icaros* with her night vision camera. The atmosphere in the room was very relaxed. It felt different from the previous session as if each person was fully comfortable in each others company. I took my position, crossed my legs, put some tissue and water within arm's reach and got ready. Otillia mentioned this was my last ceremony. I would be a warrior after this, a man ready for the world. She said that the Ayahuasca diet was a life-changing moment in anyone's life, and after tonight I would be ready. Tonight was like my graduation, and she said, "it has been a pleasure to see you grow."

Otillia lit the tobacco, taking a drag with more presence than any Don in any gangster movie, completely devoid of fear and in complete control of her mind, body and spirit. She approached me, "*Coma esta, Señor*",

"*Bien atu,*" I said, "*Bien bien*".

She said she was happy to have had me here for this time and that my fear should be overcome when all the plants and Ayahuasca had fully taken their course.

"You have to be strong and ready for this world," she said. She blew smoke around my hair three times, taking quick drags and blowing the sacred plant fumes atmospherically around me, creating a mist of mystical smoke. She then took my hands, pushing them together and blowing smoke into the cup they'd formed. Sitting in half lotus, I shut my eyes and focused on my intentions, repeating them over and over, reinforcing them with direct instructions. Otillia performed the smoke rituals on the others before returning to her rocking chair to prepare the medicine. She removed a two-litre Coke bottle of Ayahuasca from a shopping bag and put it on her small table and blew the smoke around it, twisted the top off and blew smoke and prayers inside.

Anticipation touched me.

CHAPTER 3
ALL THE BLESSINGS

I sat, knowing I was first. Again and again, I repeated my intentions. Westerners look for metaphysical or mystical insight during their Ayahuasca quest, and I was no different, striving for physiological answers and resolutions to problems, hoping for insights into my future and a connection to the spiritual world. According to people I'd spoke to, indigenous people want Ayahuasca to work for them to solve problems, restore health, and foster greater social cohesion and are not interested in the constant search we are.

"*Señor*," was called.

I was up, it felt like the most significant moment of my life. I had no nerves now though, I was so sure I would be lead home, wherever that may be. I knelt before Otillia. She poured the thick, gloopy, dark, earthy-smelling liquid into the coconut bowl. She then handed it to me. I took it in both hands, blew my breath into it three times, putting my energy and intention into the liquid, raised the bowl above my head and began to say my intentions. Life and soul's purpose, higher self, direction and creative ideas, give me what I need to go forward. I added much more detail to this whilst I knelt, ensuring no confusion. I then knocked it back in one hit, not wasting a single drop, ensuring it was all in me. Otillia handed me a tissue, and I wiped the vile-tasting liquid from around my mouth, wincing at the taste. Sitting back down, I closed my eyes and concentrated hard. I don't remember the other guys taking their medicine, I was strictly setting my intentions over and over again in my head, keeping my spine upright, paying Lady Ayahuasca the respect I now knew she deserved.

The candle was blown out by Otillia, and the waiting game began. I kept repeating my intention, focusing on staying in lotus, keeping the medicine down. It felt more settled than last time but not as settled as the first time. I sat and waited with the most beautiful expectation. Waiting to be enlightened, waiting for explanations and direction, excited by the prospect of knowing myself a little better, allowing Ayahuasca to be the gateway not for escape but for eternity, entering those worlds that live at the same time in this and other realities.

My stomach started to pulse, not liking what was inside. I reached for my bowl, but nothing came. The Lady wanted to remain. I was focused, determined to stay sat up, not let my body slip into relaxed lazy mode.

Lisa was sick, retching in a deep painful tone. Get it out, girl, I thought. Shortly after, Lucias was sick. Light visuals began, it was starting, The Lady was near, but when was I to be sick? I wanted the colour, the brilliance, the magic, time after time I prepared myself for the internal explosion that would surface through my mouth.

I held the bowl, but nothing.

I resigned myself to the fact I may not be sick, and this experience would be like my early experience of TV; devoid of colour. I decided to step inside, relax and be taken on my journey.

Like someone had been trying to prise a stop valve on a water pipe, I felt the sick race from my stomach and all of a sudden it gave way, releasing a torrent of built-up pressure. It exploded, rushing like a lightning bolt up my chest and throat. My arms reached out just in time to get the bowl in front of my mouth.

It all came up in one big hit.

I put the bowl down, leant over it and waited for more that did not come. Spitting, coughing and clearing my throat into the bowl, tying my hair back trying to avoid the sick. I drank some water, wiped my mouth, got back into lotus and allowed the most important lesson and healing of my life to begin.

I am an open and receptive vessel, I am an open and receptive vessel, I am an open and receptive vessel, I am an open and receptive vessel, Ayahuasca, teach me.

I began to see the coloured patterns again. They were not as vivid and extraordinary as last time. They were softer and felt more psychedelic, slowly melting into each other. Trees shed vivid leaves from thin branches whilst beautiful birds of paradise came in and out of focus, fluttering their spectacular patterned chests. The birds would morph from the geometric patterns that were forming mesmerising image after image. I was amazed at what the human mind could create with a little coaxing. With the left side of the brain shut down, the right side was allowed to take over. It was obvious to see where many artists got their inspiration from. It is like the valve that connects them to artistic creativity is in us all, but our valve is blocked in comparison to theirs. I'd heard that Gaudi was into LSD and this is evident from his work which shows how the altered state can create wonders that the normal mind rarely sees.

Plants and other mind-altering substances seem to be the cause of so much human growth and development. I'd heard whilst in the Amazon that many things such as language, textiles, patterns, and religions were all conceived in altered states brought about by plants.

I must have been on a similar plane to most artists. What a beautiful place, I thought. How lucky people are who can come here at will in a normal state. To be on this vibration, to be able to pick from these creative fruits at will, to pluck ideas and inspiration that float in the ether. Creative minds must be a beautiful place to spend time within. I felt like I was fully submerged in that place.

I wanted to melt into the floor and enjoy the splendour, but I kept saying, "No, you must stay upright, don't waste this opportunity, pay respect, nothing comes without hard work. Spine straight, spine straight."

In this psychedelic world of colour, art, creativity and genius, I felt safe, loved and passionate as if all my desires had been met. However, I knew that if I dropped down into that space two foot above the ground, madness lurked, waiting for my arrival, hungry to try and destroy me again. I battled to hold my body up. Every part of me was so relaxed and sitting upright was the ultimate chore.

The *Icaro's* began again; Otillia took me on a new journey.

Fhian was brought to me, this immense ball of love engulfed us, and we just sat in it. Content with each other's presence, so happy, joyful and in love and this happy contentment filled us both. She lay in my arms, resting her head on my shoulder and chest. Then we were in a hospital, she gave birth, it was so real, I was experiencing every second. This baby brought everything that had been missing in my life for the last twenty years, delivered, solved and resolved the second it entered the world. The pain and anguish of the unconditional love I'd lost six years ago in the physical form of my mother was healed. Fhian providing this for me meant that unconditional love was now between us both forever and I would worship her for the rest of my life.

Unconditional love was back in my life, I was drowning in it. The three of us were draped within it. It covered every part of us circling, dancing, jumping, spinning, like an invisible fireworks display around our bodies. The three of us were captured by this enormous love bubble, colours of energy flowing, merging and melting into us. An eternally inseparable connection was made. We were back where we'd started, Fhian on my chest and the baby on my stomach. I sat listening to Otillia's *Icaro's* with everything I'd ever wanted. I was feeling better than I'd felt my whole life. Pure joy spread across my face, the most content and happy smile must have been lighting up my mouth.

So so so so so so so so so so so so so so so so so so so happy, my mother's pride swept through me, I knew in death she could see my children always. A vision of me and Fhian's small house came to me. In the middle of the room, a chair stood with my mother's name,

Doreen, embroidered into the headrest. My two daughters were the only ones allowed to use it, unless they granted someone else permission, including me. They would go to it when they wanted a cuddle from their grandma or were feeling sad, and it would give them all the love that massive-hearted woman possessed. I thought how blessed I was to have had that love in my heart for so long and how special she must be to be able to do that from the grave. My superhero mum, who was capable of being the best grandma in the world, from her little caravan in Devon or was it, Heaven, where she now resides? Well, one of them.

Emotion swept through me. Tears raced down my cheeks. The beauty of the life I was seeing, the beauty of being shown how to tap into her special energy, my superhero legal secretary mum, who could type two hundred words a minute was there with me, and I could feel her pulsating in my heart.

That house, that wife, those blessed children of ours gave us direction, consciousness and a love that nothing else was capable of providing. I was shown my love, my family, how to reach my happiness, and how to not worry about what the world worries about. 'All will be provided for you, Liam, just trust and have faith,' was the message being sent.

Fhian looked more beautiful than ever before. We looked perfect for each other, and after our child, this new goddess-like glow filled her aura, and she became like an Atlantian priestess. I was the proudest man alive, eternally grateful to have such a great woman be part of me.

I sat in this love, in this house, with this beautiful family for what seemed like forever, I never wanted to let go. My body felt so amazing, soft and loose like I was in a world made of candy floss floating in space.

I wanted to merge with the floor, and as I slipped further and further down the wall I could see there was a lucid liquid level a foot from the ground. When my head fell and my eyes passed through this lucid liquid level crazy visuals took over; animals, snakes, birds, insects everything you could imagine were there, going nuts in this other realm, enticing me to come and have another adventure. It was all in Technicolor. There were shapes shifting into one another. Part of me wanted to sit and watch, but another part of me thrust myself back up, spine straight back to the disciplined respect for Lady Ayahuasca.

Lucias began to sing. What was happening? Was this allowed? Was he stealing Otillia's show? I don't like this change, I thought.

I wanted to be in Otillia's world, how can this work? The ceremony is going to be ruined. STOP, RELAX, SIT BACK, ENJOY & LOVE... BREATHE, BREATHE, BREATHE.

Wow, I was taken to a new place. Tingles and energy spread, making its way around my body. Love was being poured over my head like one of those wire head massage devices that look like a huge spider. Electric fluid ran down my spine. Lucias sang so beautifully, like two people were singing, like his next word came before the last one had finished and it was delivered in a different voice and tone, overlapping one another. I fell back into my dream world of love. So, so, so, so, much love, so, so many blessings, happiness exploding from my chest like a Catherine wheel. The sparks of love infected everyone they hit, everyone that saw them. I had to spread this love I was being told, like a child with too much energy.

Without an outlet I would go mad, I had to share this love, to cuddle, to hold on to people and pour my love into them, and let its infection be known to the world.

My head threw itself back, the music was pure bliss, utopia, heavenly, perfection, the rattle exploded particles of imagination through my head. The purge rushes came again, I approached my bowl on all fours, my hair down, providing a vial. More dogma and layers of unneeded baggage I had collected through life were being ripped out of me by my higher self, by my soul. It was as if the sick was coming from the bottom of my feet, where every one of these unwanted notions, memories and pains were residing. They were being forced out violently, over the overtones of the most beautiful music imaginable to man. I wretched painfully, forcing out this unwanted plethora of expectation, programming, education, TV, values, monotonous lives that we are made to feel are necessary to fit in, to be respected, wanted, valued and deemed normal by society. It was like I was in the Matrix, wanting to take the pill of truth. I wanted to be an open vessel. I wanted the falsity of parts of me to be evaporated, my ego to be destroyed, my confidence to be cemented.

I wretched again. I was eating the tasteless slop on the *Nebuchadnezza*, but it tasted better than being controlled by programmed tastes, smells and senses. It felt better to evolve than to be chastised by things I'd never had a say in.

I was never given a choice to be a meat-eater or not. Never given a choice as to whether I should drink or not. Never given the chance to choose a religion. Never given the chance of a different way of life, nationality, medical options, practices, products I consumed, cancer-giving creams, devices, products, equipment and chemicals that could have been the cause of my mother's death. I wanted to rid myself of all this, to search and be guided to the truth and be able to pass this on to my children. For them to be informed and have choices, for others who read this to think differently about what they put in their bodies and the choices they make.

I knew that telling people how they should live was not the right way, all I could do was be myself, stick to my beliefs and continue to search for the truth and listen to what feels right, not what sounds right. Our bodies know exactly what we want and exactly what is right for us, we just have difficulty listening to it.

This was in no way me belittling the way others live, it was about me being comfortable living in my body, always doing what is best for it, choosing the right foods, drinks, creams, and products. We don't put less superior liquids and oils in our cars as they would severely damage it. But most of us don't give it a thought when it comes to what we put in our bodies. All this flashed across my mind whilst trying to get my hair away from the passing sick. Still purging on all fours, I could still find beauty in the way my sweaty hair fell before my eyes and flickers of moonlight passed through the gaps in the wall and onto my face.

The music would stop and start. When it stopped, I tried to reposition my body to a respectable posture. When the music played I could only half control what it did, trying my best to not let it slip below the lucid liquid level into insanity. I was back to tapping, spreading, stretching, slouching. I was so happy, it was the best party ever. Melting and flopping, being fascinated by my limbs, the monkey in me was, here again, it always seemed present, alive.

Otillia, Lisa and Lucias were now all contributing to the musical overtures, and I was overjoyed by their abundant treat. Soon I found myself turning this whole experience into a piece of art. At first I was given ideas of how to make money in London, where I would need to live for a while if I was to commit to Fhian. I could take a 5 Rhythms-esque dance class on a Sunday morning, find a room, advertise, get a music playlist. Help people lose their inhibitions, gain confidence, get fitter, loosen up and meet new people, all with their shoes and socks off and without the aid of any narcotics.

I saw myself in East London with my van. I'd turned it into a cafe. I was serving espressos, *emoliente* and tostadas. I was learning the guitar, learning to sing my poems, and lyrics were coming thick and fast. I needed a way of delivering them, getting them off my chest.

I was then in a gallery, going through the various stages of the Ayahuasca experience, it was like an interactive performance art piece. It started off with me in a sterile white space, with my bucket and mattress going through the Ayahuasca stages, unable to control my body, but showing its freedom and bliss. The fear and the pain were visible to the audience who had their shoes off. They would ask questions, advice on their own life and be encouraged to participate in acting like a monkey. The idea evolved and evolved, a set was built like the room I was in now. The performance was called 'Ayahuasca

Monkey'. I went through each of the ceremonies. I was sick, purging, vegetable soup spluttered out from a bag on my side. I would talk about the old values and expectation, pains and confusion being shed and healed with each wretch. A life-sized model of Otillia sat rocking on one side of the room, models of the other participants stayed very still in their places throughout. A spotlight shone through the wooden cladding representing the moon, and a damp atmosphere was re-created. People asked questions in an interactive way, worried by the pain and trauma the actor (me) was going through. The gallery was full. A buzz had begun. It was all so vivid. Nothing could stop me. I was going to do it, this was my direction for now, and where I should focus my efforts, it seemed.

All the artistic stuff seemed to feel right, to flow out of me. It was telling me to focus on this and to let everything else go. To paint, to write, to sing, to act, to create, to build, to talk, to walk. This sense of freedom hit me in the face. This was the only way I would be free.

The next thing I knew, Otillia was asking how we all were. We began to chat, I talked about the love I'd been shown and the simplicity and importance of commitment and discipline, and how I would return home to my girl as soon as I left the jungle.

Otillia said, "You are ready for whatever the next stage of your life maybe". She asked how my visions had been.

I said, "Nice, peaceful, beautiful, important, but I knew the craziness was just below that line."

She said she knew. Again, she reiterated the importance of this night for me, for extra healing and focus. Lucias translated all. Then she started to tell me how my path had to be a creative one, she told me I was an artist, and I had to focus on that. I thought of when I'd read Richard Millward's book *'Ten Story Love Song'* and how the main character Bobby, really appealed to me and made me want to paint. The lifestyle, the freedom, the creative beauty of that life really struck a chord with me. In most books and films, it's the artist or musician who appeals to me the most.

She laughed at my monkey ways again, and the way my feet tapped and moved to the music, my inability to be still, the way I lay down in the living room in the days when everyone else stood or sat. "You are an artist," she said, "a free spirit, explore this more, don't worry about money it will come to you, don't chase it like the rest."

I couldn't believe what she'd said after the visions I'd just had. How did she know? How synchronised this was, it seemed serendipitous. I'd heard that the Ayahuasceros could tap into your experience like a CCTV camera watches people. This felt crazy, it was like a major reinforcement of what I'd seen. It felt magical, beautiful, lovely and right. My direction seemed set. Just be, don't push and what is rightfully yours will come. What you have been put on this Earth to do will present itself. I felt safe, warm, found, I felt clear, stress-free and happy.

The happiness I'd been searching for, for so long seemed here. I could touch it, feel it, smell it, taste it. So much joy was spreading through my veins like an anaesthetic before an operation. It wasn't just my blood and veins, it was every fibre of my being, my cells, my DNA, my organs, muscles, the water in me, every particle of me of my higher self and soul were in total unconditional bliss.

Lucias, Lisa and Otillia all spoke. I had no idea what they were saying, and I just smiled and nodded. They all began to play music together. Otillia fetched a mandolin from her room, and the music they created was divine. I closed my eyes and bounced about in other worlds as they played.

Otillia looked at me and said through the translation of Lucias, "*Señor*, you are an artist, artists can sing, sing for us!"

"Woah woah woah, oh oh no, I can't sing my voice is awful," I said.

"Everyone can sing, *señor*, it's just fear we have created around ourselves and our voice, telling ourselves we cannot or being afraid of judgement and ridicule if we let out our true voice out."

Lucias and Lisa concurred. "I bet you sing when you're alone", they said.

"Yes, all the time, but it's awful."

"You should sing, just sing a song you know," Otillia encouraged.

"But I can't, I couldn't." I was trying to think of any way out of this. "I write some songs," I said. "But I can't sing them."

"Excellent," Otillia said, "you can sing your own song." I had no way out of this, my supple body was now so tense, fear had enveloped me. There was a lot of peer pressure. On the wider scale of things, I could see they had a point with regards to me conquering my fear and becoming more confident, but I didn't know all the words to any song, and I really didn't want to embarrass myself. I thought how amazing it would be to have a good voice, I would sing all the time. I'd always imagined being the lead singer in a band would be the best job in the world. The pressure continued. I wanted a hole to take me away from this situation, but I knew there was no escaping.

"Ok," I said, "I will sing, I have a song called, '21 Souls' that I wrote on my pilgrimage for the end of the Mayan calendar." I closed my eyes, trying to find the words.

"From the heart," Otillia said, "find your voice, it's in there."

The words came into my mind. So much fear was attached to them, and my heart was going crazy. I was scared that my heart was going to beat out of my body, and I felt everyone's eyes on me. I decided to wait until I felt comfortable. With my eyes closed, part of me hoped that if I opened them everyone would have disappeared and this ordeal would be over. Occasionally the words would try and come out, but something was keeping them in, telling me to work through the blockage. I could see myself at my 30th birthday party singing the Liam and Fhian song I'd written. The voice I'd used wasn't mine, it was a voice to try and hide the real fear, a poor voice that would get the reaction of "he can't sing, but at least he had a go."

I was fully inside me, searching for these blockages, nothing else in the world existed. I was reminded of the fake voice I'd used in a best man's speech many years ago; again, it was to cover up my fear. I could see all the moments when fear had pushed me from my true self. I hadn't been me, the true me was only for the one I shared a bed with, the one I was in love with. Even my mother, the woman I loved more than all the people in my life put together, rarely saw the true, loving me.

Layers of barriers seemed to be falling from my chest. I was looking in my heart for this true voice, not just for song but for everything my true heart would lead me to. The words wouldn't come, I didn't know them. A voice said, "breathe, forget the world, find that place of comfort and bliss and when you do, just sing, it will all come."

I'd had my eyes shut for a few minutes. I hoped my wish had come true, I wanted them all to have disappeared when I opened them again. More layers and fears began to break off. I thought of how I could become another character when acting and do anything; laugh, cry, be naked, show every human emotion. Because it wasn't me, I was safe to speak in that person's voice. But as myself with no mask, I was frightened. I wanted to be brave enough to show this uninhibited true me to myself, to the world, to be full of love and not be ashamed of being so.

All of a sudden, the words just came out of my mouth, like purging but less messy. I was confused at first whether I was being sick or singing. Then I lost myself in the song. I had no idea if the words were right or in order, I just sang and sang, lingering on notes, true love and meaning being portrayed towards each person who had been on that trip in Guatemala with me. I was lost in another world, one I'd never been to before, it was a world of speech and beauty, of musical notes floating through the sky. My heart was connected to it all. I was in pure love, my heart felt big. '21 Souls lingering in the sky, ascend to the earth, ascend to the sky' reverberating in my head, overlapping with the next lines.

I finished, and tingles ran up and down my body. I wanted to cry; instead I laughed. A proud laugh of overcoming a great fear. I hoped beyond hope, I could get to this place again to make sounds like I had. I wanted to be confident in auditions, to be able to find my true voice at will and accentuate the poems of love I write with a voice to match their gentle meaning. When I had been fully in the song without worry of forgetting the words or hitting the right note, I'd seemed to be held in space and could find the note and the delivery for each word as I let it out. I felt all warm and fuzzy inside, and all the neurons in my head started to light up. It felt like sprinkles of stars were being dropped onto my head, and they were twinkling around inside. A big 'Ahhhhhh' filled my body. I melted back into my mattress as Lucias said, "Wow beautiful."

Otillia said, "See, you can, you have to keep doing this now, song can free you, can heal others."

I'd never thought of that. Then I realised we have songs for our moods. We fall in love to music, and we lose ourselves after the monotony of a week's work. It has so many uses, it keeps us company in an empty house, introduces us to the sounds we like, it's like food with people liking different types and being moved in different ways by the same taste.

I felt fantastic again, I wanted this confidence never to leave me. We all chatted like we were in our grandma's living room, laughing and joking. I asked about this monkey and baby I'd become in the ceremonies. Did the monkey mean it was my power animal? It was something I had heard quite a bit about in spiritual circles, but I had never actually had one come to me like others talked of.

Otillia said, "This is freedom of movement, your true self, the monkey is in you, it has been in you since your channel opened."

"Right then, I'm going to get a monkey tattoo, the one from the Nazca lines."

She said, "Do that, the monkey and the baby go well together, we are more like monkeys when we are children, the child in you is strong. Never lose it. We are conditioned out of that behaviour by society, parenting and a desire to fit in. Monkeys play games and have fun all the time, they are immature and like to mess around, keeping that child within alive. The only time we tend to do it as adults is when we are alone and relaxed, but as soon as someone disrupts our solitude, we tense and pretend we were not doing what we were doing. It's the human condition, you are lucky you have not lost this."

I wondered why this was. How had society and consumerism, the materialistic world not managed to enslave me? Why was I still free? Was it so I could experience more, understand more, help more people by not being locked into the system?

I always knew I never wanted it. I used to always say to friends, "There must be something better than 9-5, man, that's dry." I could never imagine going to the same office for forty years, same drive, same commute every day, hating my job, hating parts of my life. Looking forward to my two week package holiday, being so disconnected that I had to change the decor in my house every three or so years, so as not to seem cheap and out of fashion with the swarm of society. A mid-height border separating two different types of wallpaper, then the next change is a border three-quarters of the way up the wall, then back to one wallpaper, to then be discarded for painted plaster all around, then eventually a feature wall added to give more depth. Living like this would be worse than losing my mind, I thought. Please, please, please never happen to me!

I thought about why I'd always felt like I had never fitted in. Never felt a real part of any group or team. Was that again my fear of commitment cropping up or had I just never found what I needed? I always felt different from the people I knew, I cared about completely different things. Why my consciousness started to expand I have no idea, but I felt very privileged and blessed it had. Very privileged and blessed to be in this hut with Lucius and Lisa, with Guylene, with Otillia, with Lady Ayahuasca.

Lisa and Lucias played and, closing my eyes, I dropped back into the world of Ayahuasca. The singing started, and my body once again felt like pure electricity. Then I felt Otillia's energy on me, I couldn't see her face, but I felt her presence.

I sat listening, feeling Otillia working on me. Some kind of healing was taking place, I could feel it so powerfully. I straightened my spine, trying to focus and be an open vessel for Otillia's energy. I lost concentration and drifted down into the madness. Into the lucid liquid level. My slouching was almost flat to the ground as if all my bones had become mush. I reprimanded myself, "No, Browne, you must sit up, Otillia, is giving you something very special, don't spoil it." As my teachers had said throughout my life, "you have a very short attention span and don't listen". As always there was this constant battle, I could not stay focused, even though it felt like every part of Otillia was focused on me. I found myself drifting off into another thought and again would realise and snap out of it, snap my back straight and try to focus.

Part of me never wanted this ceremony to end. It had been the most powerful, meaningful experience of my life. The emphasis I had put on this moment felt fully justified. I'd always known that this would bring me some clarity, direction, trust and love. Fhian knew Ayahuasca was important to me, she had been eager for me to experience it. I thought it would give me answers and would be a huge turning point in our relationship. It felt like it was.

As I sat there, what I was going to do next flashed before my eyes. I would leave the jungle on day eight, two sleeps from now. Fly to Lima from Iquitos and then straight to Fhian. Surprise her, ask her to marry me, tell her I wanted to spend the rest of my life with her. To have everything with her, to be family, to be the most significant part of each other's lives for the rest of time, to be in love forever, to be sweet, to be soppy and an inspiration to each other. I knew part of my future was at home in Manchester, but I knew more than anything I had to make it work with Fhian in London for a while. I knew we could, I felt confident that love would conquer all, that nothing could get in the way. The clarity was like nothing I'd ever experienced before. I knew I had to get to her. I wanted her energy bound with mine. I wanted to sit and look into her beautiful brown eyes, to pretend nothing in the world existed but the two of us and that no one had experienced a love like this before. It seemed set.

I would have to wait a day before I set off. Allow the Ayahuasca to settle so I could have focus for the journey to my girl. I felt excited to want to marry someone, to want to commit, to see the beauty in commitment, to see all the new opportunities it would create, to know that I would always have someone. Someone to look out for and to always look out for me. I was ready. I'd never been so excited in my whole life.

I was snapped out of this love dream by Otillia saying again that my path looked good, looked clear, looked like there would be lots of success in all parts of my life.

She told everyone she wanted to end the ceremony soon.

She stood and glided towards me, her wide smile, revealing her white teeth that illuminated my world. With her leaf rattle in one hand she knelt in front of me. I was determined to try and convey my gratitude energetically. The *Icaro* and singing began; I was lightly beaten on my head, face, shoulders, chest and arms with the leaves. I was transfixed by the feeling of pure love, of the powerful presence of Otillia, her gentle forcefulness, my whole body vibrating, tingling, occasionally a bolt of energy would rush into my head. Pure love, peace, happiness, contentment, bliss and psychedelic joy elegantly glided and danced around my body.

I was in this other world, devoid of anything negative. Powerful healing was taking place. Otillia was doing her thing using her channel and connection to Lady Ayahuasca to pass the good stuff to me and to allow anything negative to leave my body and return to the sky.

It lasted for what seemed like an eternity, I was there, my focus was on what I was receiving. I didn't want this moment to end. Otillia's focused beautiful energy, ambient flowing words and wondrously melodic powerful beat of the rattle reverberated around my whole body. It was like standing in front of a speaker at a drum and bass rave, but more hypnotic and dignified. I felt like I was having a shamanic lesson to trust my own knowledge and capacity, to work with energy and to relax into the uncertainties and strangeness of life.

I was later told it was a special healing as it was my last ceremony and the end of my Dieta. My gratitude and love for this lady were overwhelming. She had given me the tools to be confident, to see my own beauty and stop beating myself up about all the things I had and hadn't done in my life. She'd given me what I had been looking for, had shown me the importance of true love, the fact it's worth everything and that family can change your world. Ayahuasca had fulfilled and surpassed all my expectations. Otillia, as she had said herself, was just chosen by Ayahuasca to learn about the plants and all the wonder and knowledge they hold and to show people the true nature of life. She allowed people to be cured and healed of physical and mental problems and addictions, to see their true selves. To give them direction, to see the oneness of the world and how everything that is alive has a soul and meaning. To make people see that Lady Gaia (Mother Earth) is an interconnected system we all play a role in.

Otillia and Ayahuasca seemed like a match made in Heaven. It was astounding the work they had done together, how many lives they'd changed, healing depression, addiction, mental problems, physical problems, showing so many people the light. Otillia has an 80% success rate with getting crack and heroin addicts clean.

As Otillia moved on to Guylene, she was telling me to continue this diet for fourteen days. She said to take it easy and to rest as much as I could, to sit and allow the plants to work. I said that was fine.

"Sex," I said, "can I have sex?"

This was interpreted; and smiling, Otillia looked at me and said, "*Si señor, mucho.*"

Everyone laughed, and Otillia said, "This is fine, enjoy."

I couldn't wait for my explosion of love to be cemented with this act, I couldn't wait to hold the most beautiful woman on the planet close to me and caress every part of her body. To look into her huge brown eyes and tell her that I loved her more than anything I'd ever loved. To feel the two magnets that were made in the same mould to reconnect and never part again.

Otillia finished her healing and sat back in her seat and the amazing atmosphere that had permeated the room all evening remained. Otillia asked if I would like to drink another medicine which was a final goodbye and was a plant that would stay in my system for quite a while. It would help me sleep tonight, she said. It was not an uplifting medicine. I thought it must be a natural spiritual version of the after-party drug, Valium.

Otillia said we should take it and everyone agreed. I never ever questioned it; my complete faith was in this lady. She told us we must be clean for the medicine and would have to bathe beforehand; I often did this with Valium as well if I had the energy to get in the shower.

Otillia shouted to one of the ladies who worked there and told her to fill the bath outside and make the medicine. It was the early hours of the morning, and the lady Otillia had called had been sleeping — obviously, her contract stipulated being on call during ceremonies, and I wondered if she had a beeper. I never realised there were people sleeping just on the other side of the thin wooden walls. I then thought about all the noise I had been making in that last ceremony and how I must have kept them awake.

Sleepily, she prepared the bath. Otillia said after this, I would be able to take on the world. I would be ready to fulfil my potential, nothing would hold me back, and I would have the confidence to be my true self. The bath and buckets were filled with water that I figured had been brought from the small stream close by. Flowers had typically been added, and I quickly bathed, cleansing my body under the spectacular star-studded rooftop of black glitter that ignited my vision every time I looked up. I had no towel, so it was a drip dry and then back into my ceremonial attire.

Everyone but Otillia took a bath, and when we were all clean and soaking wet, we were given a small beaker of plant medicine. Otillia said we must all drink together. After a, '*Salute*' in unison we all knocked it back. Otillia went into detail of the medicine, but my memory for things like detail always seems to fail me. I am always mesmerised by people who remember facts, I always remember weird stuff.

The ceremony was officially over. We were told we could stay and chat further and sing. Guylene needed some sleep as she had not taken the Ayahuasca. I was impressed she had managed to stay awake the whole time.

She looked at me and said, "Liam, you are a strong and powerful man, now go forth and take on the world."

A kind of gobsmacked, "Thank you and goodbye" trickled from my lips.

I stayed with the others for a little while listening to them having an Ayahuasca-filled jam session. I only lasted a couple of songs, needing some rest and wishing I could contribute. I wanted to go and be with Fhian. I imagined her in my arms, thinking about our lives together, and how I would get home to her as soon as possible. After an un-treacherous walk back to the hut and the gauntlet of getting into the mosquito-netted bed, I felt the plant medicine running through my veins. I lay back and enjoyed the love, happiness and contentedness that was creating this hazy glow around my body.

The next day I woke to this lovely world of love, calmness and manoeuvrability which hazily and fuzzily covered the mosquito net. I had one more night with Otillia. Today was a day to relax, but thoughts and plans circled my mind, it was a vast difference to the blissful emptiness I had felt the previous days. I wanted to ask Fhian to marry me as soon as I saw her. I wrote a beautiful song in my head and dreamed of singing it to her. It went like this:

John & Yoko
Will you be my Yoko
So I can be your John
Lay in bed together
Without the TV on
Sit and laugh forever
Snuggle with my honey bun
Look into your eyes
And tell you you're the one
This will last forever
I'll always be your John
And you will be my Yoko
Nothing much will get done
Laying there in Heaven
Having so much fun
Tickling and laughing
Tell each other you're the one
Planning to get married
Somewhere in the sun
I will never leave you
I won't get shot like John

I knew love was all we needed. Nothing else mattered to me, nothing else came into my head, no doubts. I lay for a while, and a creative air filled me. Poems and ideas flashed across my mind at great speed, but I had no pen to capture them. And this story circled through my mind before I actually got a pen to write it down:

To Piss Myself or Not to Piss Myself

I wake to the incessant sound of the mosquito hum and buzz. I shake in my usual way when the sound suddenly stops to see if the humming, buzzing begins again. If it does, I have company. Fortunately, via in-depth studies, my still-cloudy mind decides I'm safe. This continues for

30 or so minutes and each time I discover again the conclusion of my analysis. My body relaxes and any part of it hovering above the bed crashes back down, melting into the mattress. After another 30 minutes or so I become conscious of how desperately I have to pee, I feel like I'm in heaven though (not Devon where my mum is). The bed and my mosquito net 4-poster-esque shaped paradise shelter my need for peace and safety from all the nasties awaiting me outside. I decide to sit it out and forget about it and still feeling sleepy and induced by the plants, I'm in a mellow, marshmallow, rainbow-coloured fellows' world, and I want out. I then realise I need to pee so so so so so so so so bad that I have to escape. I also need to poo hard, and these two sensations press against the lower part of my stomach. I'm still lay flat in Marshmallow World, wishing the sensations away, discovering I could get past the feeling of my anus exploding but my penis not. I pray and imagine how cool these beds would be with a catheter so I could just piss myself. I consider pissing myself. NO BROWNE, YOU CANNOT. The monkey would, though. DOHH. Miserabled by my latest investigations findings and the poo now moving from category C to A, I resign myself to the fact I need to escape under the net and into the scary bug-infested world. My body seems destined for yellow fever, which I seemed to have avoided so far. Just putting my body through the sheer anguish that is crawling under the net, standing upright, walking to the toilet, doing my thing and then getting my notebook and pen, crawling back under my net, slapping the bugs off, hoping none have got past quarantine and lying back down seems like torture. But I have to. I turn half on my side, which is a quarter of the way towards being on my back again. My hand is holding my bum cheek, fully on the left one and delicately cupping the right. I then think of Fhian, without the hair, and get trapped in that moment for around one minute and forty-six seconds, then pull myself out and escape, going through the previously described ritual; out of bed and net stand, walk in a U shape to the toilet, lean on the wall and squat. DONE. Ahhhhhhhhhhh, clean up mess by lifting lid on huge bin of water beside, taking a small bowl, dunking to fill, removing and throwing down toilet until toilet is clear. I am being bitten this whole time, constantly slapping my ankles, clapping my hands, searching for justice from the latest culprits to have taken my blood. Crash, bang, slap, smash. It frustrates, I'm bitten, smitten, like a kitten, but knowing I'm not cos I'm a little monkey. When toilet is clear I take another bowlful, put it on the floor and like an Amsterdamian prostitute, I wash my bits there, and then, the recipe for this is twice. Then I get a fresh bowl, wash hands and feel clean to get back into bed and net, with pen and pad and write this. Sleep rest time now, with all my love. Sorry if I disgust in any way but words just flew, flowed and the new me is an artist, so I have to be led by heart and instinct. Much love and blessings. Liam xxxx

All I wanted to do was get to Fhian, nothing else mattered. I had belongings at the houses of friends I'd stayed with in Guatemala City and Miami, but that didn't matter. I thought a flight might take me via one of these places, but it wasn't imperative. All that mattered was my love. I knew tomorrow I would wake and head home, regardless of the cost. I was leaving here to spend the rest of my life with her, for us to grow together like one apple tree grafted onto another.

I thought about the things I had planned on doing in the next few months. Surfing in northern Peru, meeting my Aussie mates, building a cob house in Ecuador, more Ayahuasca ceremonies, seeing Bogotá and the pristine beaches and a country everyone raved about. Then Panama and all the Central American countries I hadn't visited yet. Then heading back to Guatemala City, the Lake, Belize and finally a week in Miami with me best mate. None of that seemed as important now. I was following my heart, all that mattered was capturing that love, catapulting us back together. Skipping through fields, making love in the long grass, chatting for hours, planning our future, supporting each other, saying this is it, you are all that I want. It was a monumental feeling, something so foreign to me, the concept I'd had all my life of how things could be.

I felt creative like an artist. I wanted to be Bobby from Richard Millward's book '*Ten Story Love Song*', but without the booze, a girlfriend who only ate sweets and living in a high-rise block of flats in Middlesbrough. I wanted not to worry about money, which seemed constantly programmed into me, but to have faith in what was shown. Put on an art piece, keep writing, work on my creativity, to keep striving to strip away my baggage, to unleash my inner child onto the world, to laugh loud wherever I went and for my healing laugh and hands to touch as many people as possible.

I wanted to achieve more in the film world, to act, to sing, to dance, to love, to jump and to run fast barefoot on the grass. To never listen to people stuck in dogma, to stay close to the true me that I had now found. To push this me to the front, to get what is rightfully mine, to fulfil my potential, to have love, have friends, to teach, to learn, to heal, to help, to support, to fully awaken, to be conscious always, to be the light and let that light shine through me.

I felt ecstatic. My heart was huge, and I was so excited to be committing to Fhian. I'd missed her so much, and I estimated that within the next few days I would be breathing the same air as her.

Breakfast was called, and Guylene was already there. She congratulated me on completing the Dieta. We ate, and Lucias and Lisa soon joined us. We chatted about the night's events. They told me how the ceremony was focused on me as it was my last and most important as it was filled with my energy and the healing was for me. Guylene filmed us all, asking how we found Otillia and our experiences. She showed me some of the footage from the ceremony, and the night vision camera had really captured the mood. I thought it would really accompany my multimedia performance piece based on the Ayahuasca experience.

I was again being bitten to death by mosquitoes as I devoured my food. Guylene was leaving soon. I loved her energy. We sat and chatted with Otillia for a while, I generally smiled and nodded. I said how amazing the evening had been, thanked her for the extra healing and focus she had put on me.

Guylene left, and we had a lovely goodbye embrace. I hoped to see her one day soon, maybe in Paris or England or maybe back here.

She was an amazing person, so uplifting, so much energy, such a warm loving nature. I felt like myself with her, she made me laugh, and my own humour poured out. I wished the amazing filmmaker goodbye and watched her disappear into the jungle. I returned to my hut, thinking about making my way to Fhian. How would I get there? I trusted it would all work out perfectly.

I tried to relax in my hammock, and for the first time I actually had to try. No Ajo Sacha this morning and the heat, humidity and dampness ensured a constant film of sweat covered my whole body. Mosquitoes were everywhere; if I was going to get malaria or yellow fever, surely this was the moment.

I went from bed to hammock several times, unable to find relaxing comfort. The makeshift net I'd put around the hammock seemed to provide little resistance to the army of mosquitoes vying for my blood. They always found a gap or a hole to get at me from, they could even bite through the material of the hammock.

When I thought I had killed the last one, I would relax into my book and, after a minute or so, I would hear the dreaded buzz again. My concentration would be broken, and I would be back on the hunt, slapping, shaking, rocking the hammock, nothing seemed to work. I was naked and stepping out of the net was like walking in front of a firing squad or throwing a piece of meat towards flies. They were on me straight away, I would spend ten minutes killing, clapping my hands, slapping my calves, shins, thighs, hamstrings, knees, everywhere was being attacked. I would swipe and clench my fists together hoping one would be inside when I opened my hand.

Then suddenly I felt something land on my penis.

Noooooooooooooooooooo! I had to act quick. Did I continue the whacking and slapping with all my might? Did I shake and hope it hadn't already locked in? I opted for a light swipe and wiggle. I inspected myself for damage, and it looked like I was in the clear.

As this had been happening, the mosquitoes had taken their chance and were preying on me from all angles. Had the penis hunt been a decoy, so my full attention was in one place? Did they know a man's major point of weakness? I realised there and then, after thinking there was nothing in the world that I hated, that actually I hated mosquitoes and wanted them to not exist.

I had used the word 'hate' flippantly for many years, and I was taught by Fhian's dad one New Year's Eve that hate was a strong word. He asked if there was anyone I truly hated in the world and wanted to see dead. There was no one I truly wanted dead, so after this important lesson, I started to erase the word from my vocabulary. It was really difficult at first, but when I said the word I would notice it and would make a point of it and say, 'No actually I don't hate them or it, as hate is a strong word'. It took six months for me to fully wean myself off using it and I had not said it since.

Until now. 'I HATE MOSQUITOES'.

Is there anyone in the world that likes them? I really do *hate* mosquitoes!

I was fidgety, distracted, hot and frustrated, and I couldn't find a place to relax. I started to think about leaving there and then, heading to Iquitos, starting this journey of reconnection a day early. I decided I was going to do it after lunch. I was free to go. I could stay another night, but it would just be to rest, something I couldn't do in these conditions.

Lunch was called, and I ate with Lucias and Lisa. We conversed about amazing, beautiful things; life, death, growth and enlightenment. Nowhere in sight was mention of jobs, cars, houses, hair, shoes and the latest trends. I found out Lucias had, had the same experience with regards to singing on his first visit to Otillia four years ago. He was put in the same situation, felt the same nervous angst and the firm belief he couldn't sing. I couldn't believe it, he sang so beautifully now. I fantasised about being able to sing like him, words coming straight from the heart. I hoped I could muster a similar sound one day soon. Lucias said he now sang all the time; music was a huge part of the healing work he and Lisa provided.

I wanted to be like this couple and live the way they did. To always be calm, softly-spoken, loving, contented and allowing yourself to be in the flow of the energy of the Universe. Trusting that all my worldly needs will be met, gaining great satisfaction from knowing that the work I do is not only helping people but pushing them towards a path of love, light, health and happiness and becoming an awakened soul.

I told them I was going to leave, to head for my girl, they said how beautiful that was and how Ayahuasca works in ways normal people can only dream of and would find difficult to fathom.

I let Otillia know and then, not in a rush but at a fast pace, frantically trying to avoid getting bitten, I scrambled like John Cleese in a wacky scene from *Fawlty Towers*, to wash pack, tidy and throw all my stuff on the grass outside to ensure minimum time in the hut and additions to my already savaged feet, ankles, and legs.

I picked up my bag, I was on the move again.

I said goodbye to Lucias and Lisa and then goodbye to Otillia, I couldn't thank her enough. I had no words, but she could see my sheer gratitude and love pulsating from my heart.

"*Mucho, mucho, mucho gracias,*" I said. I thanked all the staff, hugged the ladies and shook hands with the blokes. I hugged Otillia, praying I would see her again, with Fhian I hoped. I really wanted her to see this world. I looked into Otillia's deep eyes, taking in her energy, her presence and her stature. I thought of what I was now and what I was when I had arrived. I owed Otillia and Lady Ayahuasca so much and thought if everyone could just experience this once, if they cared about themselves, cared about being a better person, cared about being a better person for the people around them, how beautiful the world would be. What beauty there would be in this world with everyone pursuing their dreams. A re-visioning of who we are and who we want to become. To know and see the other forces at play in the Universe, at play on Earth, at play between the living, the dead, the future, the past, the spirits, the Angels, the animals, the plants. The plants that give us so, so much knowledge about how to live, breathe, heal and learn and be still. The plants that can help us see, help us be. Ayahuasca for all it does, for the thousands of people it helps every year to see their potential, their destiny, to help them heal, forgive and forget, give clear direction and remember their true self.

Our culture has vilified mystic beliefs and has historically deemed anyone who claims to be able to access other realms of reality a crazy loon. Our Judo-Christian heritage has filled us with fear of God and anything spiritual. The conquistadors of South America deemed these practices the work of the Devil and killed anyone with the slightest involvement. I hoped that our society could grow up enough to treat Ayahuasca as a doorway to the spirit world and our evolution as people and communities. I kissed Otillia on the cheek, *adios*'ed her up, flipped my rucksack on my back and headed into the jungle, unable to turn back.

I was heading for one thing now, for destiny, to start my life, it was all in front of me. The shackles I had wrapped myself in had been broken, my shoulders had lost their heaviness.

The jungle seemed more alive than the last time I had walked through it. Sounds seemed amplified, colours seemed vivid, every step was a step closer to my love. *I'm coming baby, I'm coming*, looped through my mind as I sauntered through the narrow jungle path which would be the first of many journeys I would have to tackle before I got home to my love.

A FREE 'UNPUBLISHED' POEM FOR YOU!

As a massive thank you for buying this book I would like to give you a little present. This is only for you, the people who have supported my work. I hope my experience has opened your mind to spirituality and given you something to think about.

This is a poem I recite from time to time in my yoga classes and in my Cacao Ceremonies. It seems to really resonate with people. They always say it gives them a sense of hope. It came to me in savasana in a yoga class. I couldn't get out of the class fast enough as it was fully formed in me head. I needed to write it down quickly before I forgot it.

Always know something good is coming from all negative situations. It is our task to stay as passive as possible to the dark and the light. To be non reactive. Magnificence is waiting around the corner. Move beyond you imagined limitations.

You can download the poem at - www.liambrowne.com/embrace

ALSO BY LIAM BROWNE

Books

Dealer to Healer - A Modern Tale of A Fucked Up Male

Short Stories

Hitchhiking - Feel The Good Vibrations

Poetry

Dealer Forget, Healer Remember

ACKNOWLEDGEMENTS & GRATITUDE

Massive thanks to all my spiritual teachers over the last 8 years; I owe you all my life. Most importantly I would like to show my gratitude to me mum who has guided and supported me in both life and death. You taught me so many things about being a good person and how to love people deeply. You also taught me infectious laughter and we laughed so often. Your death allowed me to look deeper and I have always felt your push and guidance. Everything poignant in my life is always dedicated to you as I understand I'd be nothing without you. Your love, warmth, generosity and kindness were so heartfelt and I am truly blessed to have you in my life every day. I know you see all I do and I hope that I'm making you proud. My father Bernard, thank you for always supporting me. Usually having no idea what you are supporting but nonetheless being there and always bringing unwavering mentalness to all situations. I don't understand you and I never will but there is something beautiful in that as you don't give two shits about what other people think. You are one of a kind. I don't think there is a person in the world who makes me laugh as much as you. You think any problems I have could be cured by eating meat and for that you are a genius. Thank you to all the characters I met on my journey, you will always be family. Massive thanks to Kathryn for starting this journey with me, to Janet for taking me under your wing and seeing potential in me. Ladan for all your wisdom, all your teaching and all your love and support. To each person who listened to my stories and said you must write a book. You are the inspiration. To Keith the Cacao Sharman, Otillia the Ayahuascero and all the spiritual teachers I have met along the way. To my editor Johanna, I can't believe I finally found you. To my designer Louise Carr, your creations always blow my mind. Thank you for putting everything together and creating the cover. Finally, to you the readers, more than anything I hope that something in this book can help you find that inner power to make some positive change and to continue to look for growth in all corners of your life. Spread love and healing far and wide. I want to help as many people as humanly possible to step into their power and remove the fear that is blocking them from becoming their finest self. FULL POWER!!!!!!!

Now sign up to me mailing list immediately! Please! That would be awesome.

Sign up here - www.liambrowne.com

Hi

Thank you so much for purchasing me book! I hope you have enjoyed reading it as much as I have enjoyed sharing my life with you. I really truly value you as a reader.

I'd love to hear your feedback on how you feel about the book. If you could take a few minutes to leave a review, I'd be so happy.

To submit your review, simply go to the books Amazon page, scroll down and click review this book.

Thanks in advance for taking the time to leave a review!

Much Love & Blessings,

Liam

SAMPLE CHAPTER

from

Dealer to Healer - A Modern Tale of a Fucked Up Male

DEALER WITH IT 2008

We crossed the border into Belgium. It was 3 am, and we were looking for somewhere to camp and get some sleep for a few hours. The roads were completely deserted, and the only light came from the headlights of the car we were driving. It seemed like thick forest flanked either side of us. In the distance we saw two red lights coming closer and closer. Finally, we were close enough to realise it was a police car.

I drove tentatively behind, not knowing what the speed limit was on this road, in this country. I travelled at a similar speed to that of the officials in front. The police car seemed to be getting slower and slower. Tired and scared, we were all struggling to make sense of what was happening as the police car slowed to an almost stop.

I decided we should go past them, so moving the car into the opposite lane, I pulled away from them slowly. As we did, I increased my speed little by little, still unaware of the country's speed limit. We got further and further away from them, and their car got smaller and smaller. A gasp of relief emitted from each one of our chests and we careered forward, away from the law.

The next thing we knew, two white lights were getting closer and closer to us. We made out it was the police again and we all panicked.

The police sat behind us for about ten minutes, our anxiety growing. Groans of, 'What are we going to do, Liam?' bombarded my eardrums.

The blue and red lights flashed on, and a doomed sinking feeling flickered through my whole body as the panicky heads of my accomplices darted from me to the police car, from me to the police car.

The flashing lights became my cue to pull over. I told everyone in the car to let me do the talking and that if worst came to worst, to say they knew nothing about it.

The officer slowly approached the car as I wound down the window in the fashion my mind had been trained to do from all the American movies I'd seen. His torch flashed into the back seat, copying all the American movies he had seen, and then it was on me.

He asked me where we were from.

I said, "England".

He asked me where we were going.

I said, 'Spain'.

He asks me what we were doing in Belgium.

I said, 'We are meeting a friend tomorrow in Bruges, and we want to find a campsite to sleep in tonight.'

He told us they would all be shut.

I said, 'We just need somewhere to put up a tent then.'

He then asked to see my driving licence and the insurance and registration details for the car.

I was not insured, and I didn't own the car. I passed him my driver's licence, and Little Blonde, who was sitting next to me reached into the glovebox for the paperwork. She was, thankfully, on the insurance, but the car was registered to a Mohammed Chowdery.

I said as little as possible and gave the police officer the papers. He went to the back of our car and talked to his colleague. We could hear him talking on his radio in a foreign language, so we had no idea of what was being said. Panicked whispers bounced around the car, and I told everyone it was going to be fine.

As one officer was on the radio, the other asked me to pop the boot. My heart sank. Everyone's hearts sank. We were fucked, or more to the point, I was fucked, and getting to the music festival in Spain now seemed unimaginable.

The officer looked in the boot, and I inquisitively looked through the rear-view mirror, trying to see what he was up to and whether he was taking anything out. I could see looks of horror saturated across the faces of my three friends in the back.

Guilt squeezed my heart.

I tried to remain calm, but the chances of coming out of this unscathed seemed as remote as the woodland surrounding us.

The other officer had a driving licence in my name and the registration details of the car in the name of an Asian man who was nowhere to be seen. In my head, this in itself justified further investigation and was a definite breaking of the law. I was not insured to drive this car, I didn't own it, and I was driving illegally in a foreign country. I knew in England I would immediately have been arrested.

He stopped talking on the radio and started a discussion with his colleague, then he turned and walked back towards my unwound window. Each step added another hundred beats per minute to my heart rate. I was ready to be taken to the station for further investigations, for the boot of the car to be searched and for my friends in the car to be answering questions their relatively protected lives may not be able to deal with.

All kinds of scenarios were going through my mind. Would I have to serve my time in a Belgium prison, or would I be sent back to England to serve my time, and what would give me the best chances of not being bummed?

The officer took his last step. His hand goes on the window trim of the door, he turned to face me as his other hand passed me back the paperwork.

He said: 'This is fine'.

I felt like I had misheard him.

In my mind, I was shaking my head in disbelief a little, quickly replaying his words again and again in my head. *He said 'this is fine'???*

Baffled, I took the papers handed them to Little Blonde next to me and looked back at the officer. He told us the speed limits of the road and then pointed us in the direction of a campsite and wished us a safe trip.

We all thanked him profusely.

Adrenaline pushed and pushed up my body until we drove off. A huge sigh of relief exploded from within me. It felt as if my body weight had halved by releasing all the tension that had built up.

Giddily, with an air of trepidation, we said things like, 'Oh my God', 'I can't believe that' and, 'Shit, wow! *Oh my God, oh my God* was repeatedly spat into hands that were clasped around our mouths as if some other entity was saying them and we were trying to keep the words from spilling out, as law-abiding atheists.

We arrived in the most picturesque of villages which, in a way, soothed the plethora of emotions we had just been through.

We found the campsite the kind police officer had pointed us towards. It wasn't open, and the chain had been put across the entrance. We decided to break in and set up camp. We only put up two tents; Little Blonde and Rena take one, and I'm left to share with Mr Japan and The Communist. The Communist is my ex-girlfriend, and Mr Japan is a friend I met at the festival in Spain the previous year. They'd had sex with each other the previous night in the same room as me dad, and now I was sharing a tent with them, and it felt a bit weird.

The next day we awoke to hear families and foreign chatter all around us. We took in our surroundings in the daylight, tried to escape without paying, but some people looked at us weird, so we did.

We arrived in Bruges where we were supposed to be meeting Mohammed, taking in the beautiful historic city and finding ourselves having lunch in one of its many squares. Little Blonde was our Mohammed connection, and we found out he wasn't having much luck getting into the country on a Bangladeshi passport.

We reflected on the intensity of the previous evening and how lucky we'd been. We were repeatedly replaying the events, trying to figure out why they hadn't seized us and the car. We came to the conclusion it must have just been too confusing or too much work for them, and we had given them a good vibe, so they let us go.

As we approached France, we ended up in a huge traffic jam.

We moved slowly towards a border control. Europe didn't have border controls between member countries anymore, and I was in shock at what I was seeing.

As we got closer and closer, we could see that cars on the other side were being searched and completely emptied. Terror filled me; it was less than twenty-four hours ago, this same terror had filled me, but now it seemed amplified. Bags and cases were being taken from the cars in front of us. They were thoroughly emptied and scrutinised. We were all in a complete panic, again I told everyone to stay calm. Inside I was far from calm. Every muscle in my body was fully tensed, knowing again that if what was happening to the cars just in front happened to us we were in a chasm of trouble. Potentially I would be spending time in a French prison.

My mind drifted as I wondered if I would be able to achieve one of my life goals of speaking that beautiful language. After a few years of being surrounded by beautiful linguistic-emitting convicts, surely I would pick it up.

Back in the room, the cars between us and the border guards were gradually disappearing. Seven, six, five, four, three, two... All the cars were let through to continue their journey. The tension was too much. We were all on the edge of our seats, sweat was dripping down my forehead, and thankfully it was a very hot day, so this could disguise my panic. Seven, six, five, four, three, two, one. The car in front stopped and its occupants handed over their passports. We watched intently. Little Blonde had our passports ready and was waiting to hand them in. The guards looked suspiciously into the car in front, which had four Asian males inside. They were asked to pull over, and we watched as the four men were taken aside to have their car searched.

We approached, awaiting our destiny.

The guard glanced at our passports...

Buy 'Dealer to Healer' - A Modern Tale of A Fucked Up Male On Amazon

Bibliography

J.C. Callaway quote from, Ayahuasca: The Visionary and Healing Powers of the Vine of the Soul by Joan Parisi Wilcox published by Inner Traditions International and Bear & Company, ©2003. All rights reserved.
http://www.Innertraditions.com Reprinted with permission of publisher.

Joan Parisi Wilcox, Ayahuasca: The Visionary and Healing Powers of the Vine of the Soul, Published by Inner Traditions International and Bear & Company, ©2003. All rights reserved. http://www.Innertraditions.com Reprinted with permission of publisher.

César Calvo, The Three Halves of Ino Moxo, Published by Inner Traditions International and Bear & Company, ©1995. All rights reserved. http://www.Innertraditions.com Reprinted with permission of publisher.

Richard Millward, Ten Story Love Song, London, Faber & Faber, 2009

LINKS

Everything Liam Browne related and all my social media links can be found via my website www.liambrowne.com. My Podcast 'Dealer to Healer' can be found where ever you listen to your podcasts, on my website and on the 'Dealer to Healer' YouTube channel. Please listen and subscribe. Thank you so much for your support.

www.liambrowne.com